© 2011 by Richard Sproul

All rights reserved. No part of this book may be reproduced, stored in a retrieval system or transmitted in any form or by any means without the prior written permission of the publishers, except by a reviewer who may quote brief passages in a review to be printed in a newspaper, magazine or journal.

First printing, September, 2011

All characters appearing in this work are real. All places and geographic locations are real.

Cover rendition by Tom Denton.

ISBN 978-0-557-68083-2

Published by AllawayBooks, Yakima, WA
Printed by Lulu in the United States of America
www.lulu.com/content/9376757

Mule Ship

by Dick Sproul,

This labor of love is
Dedicated to:

Ellen and Susan

I am Truly Blessed

Old Irish Proverb:

Your son is your son
Until he takes a wife.
Your daughter is your daughter
For the rest of your life.

I was lucky enough to have two!

The End is the Beginning

Our boat is quiet. The others, huddled under the oil stained canvas, our only shelter, are trying to sleep. I envy them. It seems impossible but I cannot remember sleeping since we abandoned ship. I try to get my mind off of the fear that I feel but do not want to admit. When successful I start to doze off but the fear rushes back, churning my belly, breaking the drowsiness, jolting me back to reality. Real sleep will not come.

I start my turn at the tiller at 1 a.m. It is now 1:30. There is no moon in the clear sky but starlight helps make out the edges where the sea and sky met. The dark outline of our sail blocks out some of the millions of stars. A light breeze barely fills it, moving our boat over what has now become a very calm sea. I turn on my light, momentarily illuminating my wristwatch and the compass and adjust the tiller to correct the heading.

Our course is due east, as it has been since we started out. I find a bright star to follow and line it up with our mast. The weather is warm but even so, I am still shivering a bit.

Today, March 9th, will be our 31st day since abandoning ship. Except for a couple of small jars of malted milk tablets our lifeboat's meager rations had been stretched out and finally exhausted ten days ago. Carefully divvied up amongst the fifteen of us at two a day the tablets lasted another four days. Since then we have had nothing. Our water ration has been reduced to a half a cup per day. We decided that any less would not help us. Our bodies are wasted. We can go another 10 or 12 days and then we will be out of water altogether. If we don't reach land that will be it.

Where is land? Where is Australia? We should have reached it days ago. How could we miss it? How could a continent just disappear? We have a good compass but which direction are we really traveling? We are pointed east but the winds and currents could be taking us anywhere.

I scan the darkness. Nothing. Only the dark sea and star-lit sky. The Southern Cross directly off to starboard. I shift to ease the discomfort of the hard wooden seat. There is no longer any flesh on my butt. It feels like my bones are pushing the through my denims, the skin about to split, the borrowed lightweight coat under my life jacket making little difference against the chilled feeling. With eyes on the star I press lightly on the tiller to again correct the boat heading.

For the thousandth time I asked myself, "What am I doing here? How did I get here?" Useless questions and I was aggravated with myself for continuing with it. But somehow the question led to scraps of memories that provided fleeting diversion. Again, going into that self-induced reverie---------------

What was that? Something had happened. Something is different. Something has changed. I stare into the darkness. Still nothing. Only the blackness of the water and the thin line of the horizon where dim stars disappear and millions of others arch over the moonless sky.

Mule Ship

by Dick Sproul,

Who lived through this experience

Prologue.

"It was the best of times; it was the worst of times." This opening line from Charles Dickens classic novel The Tale of Two Cities, certainly applied to the 1930s and 1940s. The country was beset with a terrible depression throughout the 30s and an even more terrible war in the 40s. And yet this period gave rise to what has been labeled "The Greatest Generation". Somehow the depravation, the hardships of the depression, the trials of the war, forged a tougher more durable people. People learned to face adversity, make do, innovate, invent, create, and fix things where there were few instructions and often no repair parts. Starting in 1939 and continuing through the 1940s more people were trained and educated than had ever been before.

Many were moving to different parts of the country to take "Defense Work" jobs. Young men had to register for the Draft. Women who hadn't worked in years or maybe not at all were trained as riveters or machinists. When even their foreman was called to fight they had to step up and be bosses.

In spite of all the hard demanding things that were happening, people had fun. Not everybody had a telephone so "dropping by" was encouraged. "Stay for dinner, we have plenty," even when it wasn't really true. Dance halls were in. Swing dancing, jitterbugging even square dancing and ballroom dancing. All drew huge crowds. Everyone had their favorite Big Band. Hardwood dance floors a quarter of an acre or more in size sprang up across the country. When defense industries began working three shifts a day swing-shift dances starting at midnight became popular. Nearly everyone belonged to a bowling league. Some belonged to several. Every neighborhood had a busy movie theater showing a double feature, a cartoon and the latest newsreel of events. In the 30s the news was about long bread lines or the Oklahoma dust bowl. Every time former President Herbert Hoover appeared, loud "Boo's" were heard. President Roosevelt was often cheered. In 1939 news about the war in Europe dominated both newsreels and newspapers, with the Democratic-leaning Los Angeles Times supporting Roosevelt with his Lend-Lease program to help England. The Republican-leaning Los Angeles Examiner carried columns by Westbrook Pegler taking a strong isolationist view and calling Roosevelt a "War Monger."

In sports news, baseball was king and college football and basketball games were also drawing huge crowds even though most of the best players soon joined the military. It wasn't long until the military academies fielded the best teams.

During this time millions of boys were coming of age. I was lucky to be one of them.

.

Mule Ship

Part I

We Meet

*W*ith still a bit of Southern California twilight we pulled up in front of the security gate. It was December 27, 1944 and I had spent Christmas at home. A very dim light bulb under a hooded reflector, as required by the wartime dim-out, barely illuminated a sign indicating access to Piers 43 to 54.

My Union orders directed me to "Pier 52, Terminal Island". Dad turned off the dimmed out headlights of our 36 Ford and flicked the ignition switch down to kill the engine. He had used a bit of precious rationed gasoline to get me to my destination. A uniformed civilian security guard stepped out of a small shack set just inside the chain-link fence to let us know that he had observed our arrival. An older fellow, he was nevertheless alert and watchful. The fence was topped with strands of barbed wire and stretched off into the darkness. Inside the shack I could see a telephone alongside an opened copy of The Saturday Evening Post. Without a word we both stepped out of the car. I opened the back door and pulled my white canvas seabag off of the back seat and set it on the ground. I reached back a second time, grabbed my P-Coat and slipped it on. Being a typical December Southern California evening it wasn't that cold, but it would be easier to wear it than to carry it. Dad came around and for a moment we stood there looking towards the huge warehouses that blocked our view of the harbor. The last item on the back seat was the emergency kit suggested by the

Dick Sproul

trainers at the Maritime School on Catalina Island. I had purchased a small cheap canvas bag and put in a pack of chewing gum, a spare whitehat, a toothbrush and a set of long underwear, all recommended items for survival at sea.. A small red booklet with the title, "Safety For Seamen--Any Fact May Save Your Life" was also in the bag. With the war winding down it's probably a waste if time bringing this along. But it's my first trip and so I'm following all directions.

"Well, I guess this is it." I said. Dad stuck out his hand and we stood there a minute. Then, uncharacteristically, he pulled me closer and put his other arm around me. Up to then I had been completely absorbed with thoughts about the new adventure I was about to begin and for an instant I didn't know how to react. I had already said my goodbyes to mom before we left the house. She was going to come along but at the last minute she begged off.

I could see the tears building up and I knew she was going to cry after I left. The family had a pretty good Christmas with only my brother absent. Gene was now in France but apparently out of harms way serving behind the lines as a MP. After over a year of guarding German prisoners in Texas he had finally been sent to Europe where Allied forces were closing in on Germany.

"Looks that way" he responded after a minute. "Is there any chance you can get home again before your ship leaves?"

"I don't think so. I'll ask but the guy at the union hall said this ship was leaving pretty quick"

"Are you really a union member now?"

"Yeah, all merchant marine crews are. You have to join the Sailors Union of the Pacific or the National Maritime Union to sail on any American ship. They just call them the SUP or the NMU. It was part of the agreement I signed when I joined the U.S. Maritime service. I didn't have any choice.

Mule Ship

> **SEAMAN:** This is the stub of a form which is sent to the Washington Office of the Recruitment Manning Organization. This form is the basis of obtaining and maintaining your draft deferment. You should take up any draft board difficulties with your union hiring hall, with the personnel office of the steamship company, or with the port office of the Recruitment and Manning Organization. **IMPORTANT:** You are to reship by the "Date to ship again." This date was calculated by allowing 2 days ashore for every 7 on ship, with a minimum of 4 and a maximum of 30 days. If you are between the ages of 18 and 65, be sure to keep your draft board informed of your address or you may be declared delinquent and be classified 1-A.

Note on reverse side of Union pay stub

After the training school I was discharged from the Maritime Service and sent right over to the NMU. That's the way it works. I have to take whatever assignment they give me." I didn't want to tell him that this first assignment was as a bedroom steward taking care of officer's quarters.

"I've never belonged to any unions," He stated emphatically. "They just cause problems."

"Yeah, there were a few rough looking guys hanging around the Union Hall, some of them behind the counter. But," I added, "A lot of them were kind of pathetic too. Some looked like they just came from skid row. But most were just ordinary guys, most older than me. I wonder what the crew of this ship will be like?"

"You stay clear of trouble, OK?"

"OK dad, I will."

I turned, shouldered my seabag and headed towards the huge dark warehouses now outlined by the fading light in the west. I looked back. Dad was standing there by the guard shack. I waved. I couldn't tell if he saw me. I waited in the darkness while he started the Ford, turned back and disappeared into the night.

Between the buildings I could now see the ship. With my sea bag on my shoulder I moved past the corner of a warehouse and its full length came into view. Just a dark silhouette. Back-lighted by the rapidly diminishing traces of twilight it almost looked fake, like it was cut out of cardboard. But Huge! It was a Liberty Ship. We had studied them at the Maritime School. Of course, there was the stack, topped with that strange collar giving it, to me, a rather stupid look. Like a stiff beret perched on a large pipe. What was already a homely design made even more so by this feature. A blunt bow and single continuous deck contributed to it's ungraceful look. I could make out the gun tub on the bow and smaller gun tubs up on the flying bridge. Half way down the deck was a large life raft tilted up on rails. I knew there were others aft and on the port side.

Something was different about this ship. I could make out the gun tubs but the shape of the deck was different. Was the ship already loaded with deck cargo?

Mid-ship was a gangway also lit with dim hooded lights. On deck was a lone white-hat sailor wearing a pea coat and a webbed garrison belt. One of the navy gun crew no doubt. Was that a 45 caliber on his hip?

"Richard Sproul--I've got orders." I fished out the papers from the union hall, The National Maritime Union or NMU as everyone called it. He studied them for a minute under the light.

"OK, go aft, cut across to the port side, through the bulkhead door and forward to the Pursers Office. Check in with the Chief Steward there."

"Uh, what are those wooden structures on deck?"

"They're mule sheds." he responded. "The Chief will tell you all about it"

Mule sheds?

Following directions I found the door with a small plaque, Chief Steward on it and below that, Purser. I knocked. I heard "Come in" and opened the door. There was a bunk on one side and a desk on the other. A white sink under a porthole separated the two. A swivel chair anchored to the deck and a couple large filing cabinets filled the rest of the room.

Mule Ship

He said his name was Louis Dufore, looked at my papers signed me in and showed me to my quarters.

Moving down the passageway, "Good, now we have a full crew, you're the last man aboard," he offered. He also informed me that the entire deck crew was straight from the Catalina training school. *I wonder why that is?*

"You might know some of them." Then added, "Since we have a Chief Mate and a Chief Engineer don't call me Chief." He cautioned. "Louie' will do just fine."

That was a good sign. He seemed to be a regular guy. I didn't ask him about the mule sheds.

At the last room before the outside bulkhead door I had just came through he stopped and knocked and went in.

He introduced me to the two already getting ready for bed. I took the unused top bunk. "I'll see you in the morning."

The next morning, after a quick knock the foc'sle door opened. Louis, leaned in. "OK Sproul, have I got that right? Sproul? time to get you started. Get dressed and meet me in my office."

I laid there for a minute remembering where I was. It was 6:30. Through the porthole I could see dawn breaking. I jumped out of my bunk put on a shirt and pants and laced up my boots. Down the passageway I stop for a minute in the head and do what I have to do. The head is a small steel cubicle with a toilet and sink. The wooden door has a kick-out panel at the bottom just like the mock-up doors demonstrated in one of the classes on Catalina Island.

At his desk he went over the ship's personnel. "At the moment we have fifty two people aboard. Twenty seven Merchant Marine and twenty five Navy Armed Guard." He went on. "In a few days one hundred soldiers will come aboard and load over three hundred mules."

Dick Sproul

I had some of experience with horses but the only mules I'd ever seen were in farmer's fields pulling plows. Three hundred mules is a lot of mules! I thought about this coming spectacle. Where are we taking them and how do they load them I wondered? And where did they get them?

"The GI's quarters are in cargo hold number three. The mules will be in stalls in the main deck and on the t'ween deck in holds one, two, four and five. The GI's will take care of the mules. Fifty of the GI's are actually called Cavalrymen. Come on, now that it's light I'll give you a quick tour."

Out the water-tight door we take the ladder to the boat deck.

The long structures I had seen the night before were obviously the stalls. Made of wood and painted the same color as the ship. Planks and hand rails on top made up a catwalk to the bow and the stern gun tubs. I identified the five inch gun on the stern and a three incher on the bow. On each corner of the flying bridge there was a twenty millimeter cannon pointed straight up out of their gun tubs. At Catalina I had practiced on one just like these.

Well, not really. Class-room study sure, but when the section marched passed the small palm trees to Catalina's Casino Point to actually fire a weapon it was classic. A canvas cover was pulled off a 20 mm cannon, it's three foot round base bolted to the cement about fifty feet from the Casino. The fifty round magazine was readied and the big six foot four instructor demonstrated again how to attach it, get into the shoulder straps and work the trigger lever. Lined up according to height the shortest guy in front stepped forward and took his place at the gun. The plan was that each student would fire three to five rounds and then the next one in line would do the same.

"Just to get the feel," he said.

There were eight guys ahead of me and I was excited and eager for my chance. But there was only the one full ammunition magazine authorized and I hoped no one would freeze up and shoot more than their share. The instructor reached forward and pulled the breech lever back sliding the first round into the chamber.

At that moment a lone seagull appeared, lazily flapping its wings about 50 yards out. The instructor grabbed the little guy by the shoulders. "Start firing!" He yelled. Pow-Pow-Pow the tracers arced out, bracketing this 'target-of-opportunity'. "keep firing!" The instructor using the student's shoulders as handles skillfully maneuvered the weapon.

It still seems impossible but that bird stopped in mid air and actually dodged those bullets. I could see the tracers and it seemed he could too. The fifty rounds went out and the gun fell silent. With frantic wing flapping and some kind of bird gymnastics he didn't lose a feather and then continued on his way,-----as though this kind of thing happened every day. So much for my chance.

The Maritime School on Catalina had presented me with a mixture of learning, marching, exercise, new friends and only one stint on KP. The screw-ups of course saw plenty of KP but I managed to avoid it the rest of the time. It was as close to being in the military as you could get. By brothers admonition to, "Don't get in the army!" came back to me. He hated basic training and that was almost the first thing from him after his first leave home. Six hours getting the basics of seamanship, tying knots, various types of weapons, ship nomenclature and first aid, and a couple of hours marching on the "Grinder" each day and, lets face it, I was in the military!

I had taken the Red Cross first-aid course during my stint as a theater usher, and sailing in Newport Harbor along with vocational courses in high school. That and the rigorous training for football, made it all rather easy. What was so surprising was that many others in my section had so much trouble. Where had they been? I came to the conclusion that my "C average" intelligence meant that there were more dumb people out there than I thought. This wasn't so bad! I was rather enjoying it. Except of course marching on the 'Grinder,' the daily inspections and being a bit homesick was the down side. Aside from that we were treated pretty well, and you couldn't beat the scenery of Catalina beaches and view. No girls however! The few families still on the island had apparently sent their children elsewhere.

Actually, I was more than a bit homesick. Saturday night shows at the Catalina Casino, usually a movie but a couple of times USO shows made the whole time pass a little quicker. One of these nights a big band played and featured a new singer introduced as Perry Como. I hadn't heard of him but he was pretty good!

The day came when we had to prove we could swim. They said it was required. But it was December for Gods sake!

"So?" came back to us. "You think ships don't sink in winter?"

We gathered at the small lagoon the other side of the Casino Point wearing only our issue swim suits, T-shirts and heavy P-coats. One shivering fellow said he couldn't swim at all. Didn't matter, our section leader muttered a few choice words, ripped off his own coat and T-shirt, gripped him under one shoulder and with strong strokes dragged the quivering guy across to the other side.

"There! You can swim!" he announced.

Weak swimmers who took so long getting to the other side came out shaking and barely able to walk. They were quickly toweled off and hustled back for their clothes. Me, I did my best imitation of a water bug crawling on water, keeping my body as far up as possible---without much success, God it was cold! Bolting out of the water and up the other side I grabbed a towel and ran back in the freezing air to the starting point where my clothes were.

That coat felt so good!

Christmas was approaching as was our formal discharge from the Maritime Service and re-assignment to one of the merchant marine unions where we were obligated to take the first job offered. The alternative was immediate return to draft status, 1-A.

I sure didn't want to go through another Boot Camp!

Chief Steward Louis Dufore continued, "I want to stress that there is ammunition stowed at the bow and the stern so there is no smoking near those areas as well as the flying bridge," brought me back.

"I don't smoke" I said

"Good, I think you know where the life boats are. Your station is number one boat on the starboard side." I have to remember that, I note, my Catalina Island Maritime School training kicking in..

"Your battle station is to assist the gunner on the forward twenty millimeter on the starboard side." Another thing I'm sure I won't forget.

"OK let's go inside and I'll show you your duties but first I have to introduce you to the Captain." We made our way to the Captains quarters. His knock elicited a quiet "Come in."

We stepped in. "Captain, this is the new bedroom steward, Richard Sproul. He came aboard last night. We have a full complement now." He added, "this is Captain Dennis"

"Glad they finally got us somebody. What do you like to be called, Richard or Dick?"

"Well, usually everybody calls me Dick." He puts out his hand.

"OK Dick, glad to have you aboard. Where are you from?"

"I'm from LA---ah, Los Angeles" I manage to blurt out.

Dick Sproul

Captain Dennis was good size, a bit taller than I and a sturdy build. Maybe a bit on the heavy side, dark hair and eyebrows, even features. About 30 years old I guessed. His quarters include a small office with a desk and chair. Above the desk is a felt-lined polished wood bracket securing a gleaming brass sextant. Through the open door I see a bedroom and a separate bath with shower. In the bedroom is a basin, a towel rack and a low chest. The top of the chest has a green leather pad and also serves as a bench. A locker stands next to the basin. There's a small nice looking desk nestled against one bulkhead. A half open sliding door reveals a clothes closet about four feet long. Civilian clothes and a Dress Uniform are visible. There are two portholes looking out onto the boat deck. Dark green curtains can be pulled over the portholes. Altogether it is a rather pleasant place with some dark wood paneling and light sconces on the bulkhead. Pretty nice quarters for a wartime ship.

"Again, glad to have you aboard. Thanks Chief."

Recognizing we are being dismissed, Dufour leads me out. "Your day starts at 6 AM and you have to make up the First Mate's and the First Engineer's quarters before they come off the 4 to 8 watch. You will have to make up the Captain's quarters once a day when he's not in there. Be sure and knock before entering. He usually starts his day on the Bridge at 7:30 so you have to take care of things then. After that you can take your breakfast break. However it's customary to wait until the four to eight watch get their chow before you get yours."

Next we visit the Chief Engineer and the First Mate's quarters, somewhat less luxurious than the captains but still not bad. Then the quarters for the 2nd and 3rd Mates and their counterparts from the Engineering Department. We also met the navy Armed Guard officer who was bunked in with the 3rd Mate. Two bunks to a room with basins between the bunks and they all share couple of showers and toilets. All quite Spartan but still a lot nicer than the crew quarters where there are four bunks to a room and not even a basin.

"OK, here's the way it goes. You will have to schedule servicing the rooms to when each watch is on duty. If you work it right you can get it all done in five or six hours. Actually it's not a bad job. At the end of voyage it is customary for the ships officers to tip the bedroom steward, that's your title by the way. Some even think it's the best job",

I thought about this. Most of the crew had to stand two four hour watches as well as maintain the ship during daylight hours. Still, being a damn chamber maid was not how I wanted to spend the war.

He went on explaining details where the linen closet was, I had to change all the sheets and pillow cases each week. Towels too, unless they asked for fresh ones, which they could do at any time. Toilet brushes, cleaning supplies, mop and bucket, were all in another locker on the bridge deck.

"Take all the dirty sheets and towels down to the ship's laundry. You can drop off your stuff there too. Socks, shorts, dungarees and things.. You are entitled to laundry service once a week. Sometimes more often if something unusual happens. Our laundryman takes care of it.

Things could be worse. And what is something unusual?

Dick Sproul

The Departure- December 31, 1944

Leaving on News Years Eve was tough. Our ship, moving slowly, passed the darkened Los Angeles Harbor lighthouse standing at the end of the breakwater. Behind us dark shapes of other ships riding at anchor. All exterior lights were extinguished and portholes dogged closed or deadlights installed. These devices allowed air to enter through black louvers while blocking all light. My first wartime trip on the open sea. Leaving the calm harbor waters I could feel the ship roll as the ocean swells had their effect. The weather was mild even on the last day of the year, the Southern California reputation holding. Standing on the deck wearing my P-coat I watched all traces of land disappear. It was somehow kind of eerie. A sense of watching the world slip away.

My world now. So this is what homesickness is really like. My visit to Cousin Bob's ranch in Oregon didn't produce this feeling. I thought about my friends at the party. Boy! I'd rather be there than here. At midnight I would be kissing all the girls. They seemed to like it and I know I did! I had heard about couple of other parties and if I played it right I could have made it to more than one. You never knew when you might meet someone new. Someone with the look. Someone that had that sparkle in her eye and would move in close. I loved that!

But now I was here on this ship and someone else was moving in on those girls instead of me.

Mule Ship

Pacific Crossing

*N*ine days out, and for awhile we can get Hawaiian music on the ships radio and put out on the P.A. system. This has been a nice touch and helps allay the growing homesickness, boy, it would have been nice if we could have put in there! No such luck! But now, in a way, I'm getting used to life at sea, and it stinks! And I don't mean just from the mules. It's boring. Kind of like being in prison. I don't have much in common with most of the merchant marine crew even though all of deck crew had, like me, just come from Catalina School and only one was from Southern California.

Every day we would see ships on the horizon, usually freighters or tankers. Once a ship that looked to be a destroyer paralleled our course for a while then disappeared. The radio music fades. Occasionally the Chief Purser puts a record on the intercom but mostly there is just the gentle rolling of the ship and blue skies and a few puffy clouds to provide the days excitement. In more direct words, I am bored! The deck crew and black gang have their watch to stand, four on and eight off. I have my duties looking after the ships officer quarters. Up at 5:30, finished by noon. Day after day that's it! Each day seeming longer than the day before, not just because we are getting closer to the equator but because of the tedium. Most of the crew and the navy gun crew, and the GI's too, are outgoing and easy to talk to and that helps, but I'm just plain getting homesick.

The air moving across the deck gets hotter and ever more humid but it's the only breeze we have. Our

Dick Sproul

passengers, the 100 GI's, now spend most of their time on deck in government issue T- shirts trying to stay cool. The GI's are ordered to wear their life jackets whenever on deck, just in case one of them falls overboard. Some try to leave T-shirts below but are quickly yelled at by one of the sergeants or one of the army officers. And of course we are at war. The boat deck, with the four life boats is off-limits to the GI's and often has two or three of the army officers and some of the ships officers leaning on the rail shooting the breeze. The Army officers, two captains, one of them a doctor, and two first lieutenants are taking their men, and their animal charges, 317 Army mules, first to Calcutta, I am told, and then over the Himalayas to Burma for the campaign against the Japanese now occupying Indo-China.

I had watched the loading of those mules two days after coming aboard. It took several hours. Each mule, young, probably less than two years old, carefully groomed and well fed. Magnificent animals, each lead by a soldier with a close grip on the halter, down a ramp from trucks lined up on the dock and moved up a special gangway onto the deck and then down into stalls built in the ships holds. After securing the animal the soldier would come trotting back down a separate gangway to fetch another mule, finally filling the stalls on the main deck. I wondered where they all came from.

Somebody must have had every jackass in the country doing what jackasses do. Talk about your war effort! Previously loaded were what seemed to be hundreds of bales of hay and sacks of other animal feed. Stevedores worked the steam winches with impressive coordination, reeling out one cable while reeling in the other. The two cables hooked to a cargo net raised the load, first straight up and then quickly over the deck to the open hold where it dropped neatly down to waiting men. The net was unhooked and reattached it to an empty net for a return trip to the dock to be filled up again. This process went on for hours and included other supplies needed for war.

Dick Sproul

18 Days Out

*I*t's Jan. 18th.----18 days out into the Pacific. Heading south by southwest towards Melbourne, Australia, our first port of call, still eight or nine days ahead of us---then on to the Indian Ocean and Calcutta. I eagerly anticipated seeing things I had only read about. I wondered what Australians are like? Do they really say "Ga-day mate" as the US Navy gun crew sailors said?

How much time will we have ashore? Will I get to see lots of kangaroos? What will the people of India be like? What about those Untouchables and sacred cows?

The only breeze across the deck is created by our moving ship. No clouds, no birds hovering on invisible thermals as we had seen on other days. A high thin overcast muted the full sun. The humidity and heat confirming that we are now well passed the equator and in the southern hemisphere. Summer in January, that's going to be weird. Huge smooth swells make up the ocean's surface but are quite different than those we had seen before. Much larger and not rippled in any way by the wind, as the sea had been yesterday and all the days before. It was as if some giant hand had taken the skin of the becalmed ocean and given it a mighty snap. There is no texture; it is steel colored, smooth, glass-like except for these long huge undulations. Fifteen feet or so in height, 50 feet or more between the troughs. They were awesome. Without a reference point they seem stationary as our ship cuts through each one, our course almost at right angles to the length of the waves. What could cause such waves if the wind did not? Some distant storm?

Mule Ship

Or perhaps an underwater disturbance of the earths crust? With some of my shipmates we chat about this.

Now and then a flying fish punctures this perfectly smooth surface, exiting from one side of one of these water canyons and then soaring across the trough and disappearing into the next. A few of these amazing fish actually make it over the hump, gracefully sailing on to the next wave before knifing back into the water. One seemed as if he was actually going to make it clear over the second wave, and we cheered him on. But no, too bad, he skidded into the very top of the wave.

Are they doing this for fun? Or are they escaping some predator? More likely the latter. In any case it makes entertaining viewing for the crew of the *S. S. Silvester*, a Liberty Ship launched two years earlier in 1942, by California Shipbuilding Corp, Los Angeles CA.

Standing in the shade of the ship's bridge and leaning on the railing with Jack Funk, he was the only one I knew that was from southern California, and Jim Cox, two of the deck crew. Down on the main deck several soldiers were lolling about smoking or talking and probably just as bored as we were.

I frequently visited their quarters down in the number 3 cargo hold just forward of the bridge. A huge cavern of space filled with over a hundred bunks of canvas stretched over steel pipe hinged to stanchions between the overhead and deck. The Army Galley and dispensary areas were walled off from the bunk and mess areas. Four long tables and benches, all bolted to the deck, made up the "mess hall." A wide steel stairway much like a subway entrance connected the hold with the main deck. In the center of this space was a large opening to the lower cargo hold. This 'cargo hatch' as all other cargo hatches was closed over with long steel beams and heavy metal-banded oak sections. Covering this was a thick canvas cover secured around the edges to complete the water tight integrity of the hold.

Dick Sproul

Several soldiers were always lounging on the hatch playing cards or just shootin' the bull. I debated with myself about mentioning the warning received during my Catalina training about being on the hatch covers during wartime. Surely the army had been told and were just ignoring it.

But here on the boat deck we were content to just watch the sky and the sea and feel the slow smooth movement of the ship. Jack was a tall, thin guy, quiet and polite. Cox was short and sturdy looking, pugnacious might apply and also, I suspected, younger than he should be to be on this ship. For some reason the 1st Mate selected him to be Boson's mate, effectively the foreman of the seamen.

It had to be an acting title since this was the first trip for all of the deck crew however this is what the Union Hall sent over and the 1st Mate had to make the best of it.

Only a slight bump as the blunt bow parted each smooth crest and occasionally a small vibration from our propeller breaking clear in the trough brought the reality of the ship and the ocean to us. The light, hot breeze created by the ship's movement felt good on my face.

For a moment I contemplate the wake of our ship, our bow wave fanning out each side, making a disturbance visible on to the horizon behind us. Each of those waves now showing a pattern moving across the row-like dips and valleys. Usually our wake would start to be mixed into the surface of the sea by the wind ripples and after a mile or so be invisible---not so today. A submarine passing miles behind us would be able to see the pattern and track us. At only ten or eleven knots we would be easy to catch. A sub on the surface could easily make twenty. But from all I had heard, the Japanese Navy, or what was left of it, was girding to fend off invading Allied forces now closing in on their island nation, far away from where we were. More to the point, we were informed we were now passing through what was called 'a combat zone' and get a bonus of one-half pay added to our base pay. I guess this was one other good thing we could thank the Union for.

Let's see, one-half of our monthly pay divided by 30, times the 2 days in the zone is what? About a dollar added?

A loud ROAR from above and I freeze, white knuckles gripping the rail.

A plane just clearing our masts, blocking the sun for a blink-----a US Navy PBY patrol plane letting us know they were around. I'm sure that they knew they had scared the shit out of us.---- me anyway. Great sport for the pilot and crew I supposed. The plane soon disappeared over the horizon leaving us alone again on this strange day and strange ocean. Anyway my apprehension about submarines diminished.

Cox and Jack left to go on watch and I was left with my thoughts. What am I doing on this ship, moving across this immense ocean, stretching clear back to home?

It is getting late in the afternoon and the GIs will be cleaning up after the mules soon. They do this every day in preparation for the garbage dump at dusk and I would rather be inside when that happens. Not that it's that bad, and they always turn the ship into the wind but its still better inside. I had learned on Catalina Island that enemy submarines could track a ship by following a trail of garbage, so dumping it all at once at dusk made sense. Even so the combination of kitchen and mule buckets all being carried aft and dumped, well, I just wanted to be out of range. There was always that chance of an errant gust of wind. Actually with so many soldiers looking after the mules things were kept pretty clean. Sometimes, whenever I had time, I would stroll past the stalls and admire these fine animals. Always brushed and clean with glistening coats which I took to mean they were well fed. I liked rubbing my hand over their soft velvet noses. All in all, the mules, as a cargo and with the care they got, the bad impression implied at the union hiring hall about this ship seemed unfounded. I must have read too much into

Dick Sproul

the previous deck crew's refusal to sign on for another trip. There must have been another reason for all of this deck crew being straight from the Maritime School and of course on their very first trip, same as me.

Pearl

*L*and! One morning, there it was, Australia. At first just a low dark strip on the horizon, then in late afternoon of the next day we steam into the harbor. In the distance Melbourne didn't look that much different than L.A. Quite a few six and eight story buildings. It seemed that every G I aboard was lined up at the rail hungry for Liberty. Disappointment was vocalized when the anchor chain rattled as the anchor was released. We had to stay in the middle of the harbor until a docking space became available.

Anticipation of going ashore showed on everyone's face. "Channel fever" it was called by the old timers but they had it too. With the ship at rest my duties stayed about the same while the rest of the crew had more time on their hands. Card games erupted everywhere. A few books were opened up to be read or traded. A couple of the older guys decided they wanted to fish. They pestered little Jim Cox the Bos'n to let them have one of the fishing kits out of the life boats. Jim refused, emphasizing that they were a part of the emergency gear in every boat.

As the twilight dimmed the few office lights we could see started to go out to comply with war time rules. Along the harbor edge a few lights still flickered as activities there had to go on. Car lights appeared occasionally but they too were dim.

Later I spotted a couple of figures leaning over the stern with a fishing drop-line. They must have found some gear after all. I dismissed the thought that I should tell the Bos'n about it. No sense in stirring up the little guy.

Dick Sproul

Next morning the anchor came up and a tug boat came alongside. I rushed my tasks with the understanding that I could go ashore when finished. I did take the time to watch the docking. Heaving lines were tossed to a couple of dock hands waiting our arrival. The ships hawsers were quickly pulled over to the dock and flipped onto the huge docking bits. Our deck crew cinched up the hawsers with the steam powered winches drawing the ship snugly to the dock. All of this under the direction of the First mate, standing on the starboard wing of the bridge.

"Take in the forward spring line," he commanded through a megaphone. Then "Take up on that outboard line." The Second and Third mates standing on the bow and the stern supervised the inboard and outboard lines threaded through openings at the ships rail and on to steam winches. Fore and aft lines were reeled in and the ship nestled up to a dock lined with old rubber tires hung there to protect the ship's hull. The buildings of Melbourne not too far off in the distance.

I hurried back to work to get everything done and catch up to some of the guys but by the time I finished all of the crew except for those needed to secure the ship had gone ashore. I pulled on some slacks, black shoes and a dress shirt and contemplated wearing my letterman's sweater I had brought along just to show off. Discretion prevailed and besides it was kind of warm. I reported to Louie, the Chief Steward in his office and signed for a draw. He handed me twenty Australian Pound notes and some coins.

"That should be plenty" he said. "These are worth almost four American dollars. The last time we were here the rate was three dollars and eighty three cents." He added a quick explanation of the coins and their value, most of which I had already learned from guys who had made previous trips. Several Florins, two shilling coins that could be pounded and filed into rings were included. When in port the tap-tap-tapping could often be heard and when the center was drilled out the finished product proudly displayed.

I had heard that British pounds were worth over four dollars but didn't dwell on that and headed for the gangway. There was one of the Navy Gun crew standing guard, that forty five on his hip. He waved me on. Heading towards town I was feeling a little left behind. Still, I could understand everyone was in a rush to see what waited for them in this Australian city.

Walking alone I noticed war posters, just as at home. Most of the people I passed gave me little notice and looked not too different than people at home. The few men in sight wore soft cloth caps and dark vests over thin long-sleeved shirts. There were no young men. The women's dresses were longer than back home and somewhat plain.

Up close Melbourne looked not that much different than Los Angeles. A bit smaller perhaps but several five or six story buildings clustered together looking a little smudged just like LA. Of course I expected to see cars driving on the left side but it still seemed strange to see street cars also going up the left side. But how could it be otherwise? And there were fewer cars. Even with gas rationing there were a lot more cars on the streets at home. I sure wasn't in Southern California anymore.

Something else seemed different, almost as if I had jumped backwards in time. California was new, fresh, growing with lots of new buildings and people dressed in the latest styles, not that I was an expert. Here there were no new buildings. Stores and shops and signs were somehow like those I recalled years ago in Los Angeles.

It quickly dawned on me, England and the British Commonwealth, which included Australia of course, had been at war since 1939. Rationing had started here years earlier. While America was booming, particularly Southern

Dick Sproul

California, people here were cutting back. In early 1942 Australia seemed in danger if being invaded by the Japs while earlier in 1939, 40 and 41, we were building huge Aircraft plants. Douglas, Lockheed, North American and several other newer companies were expanding three, four, or more times. The whole south side of Mines Field, the main Los Angeles Airport, and over into adjacent El Segundo, was now covered with massive aircraft plants.

New restaurants, stores and housing tracts sprouted up to support these factories. People were pouring in to get "Defense" jobs. I noticed snazzy new night clubs in Hollywood and USO clubs being built for military people on leave. The huge new Douglas satellite plant built at Long Beach airport, the large Hughes Aircraft plant, across from the original Douglas plant at Culver City airport as well as the Lockheed Aircraft installation in Burbank were all built or expanded in 1940, 41 and 42, and spurred growth all around. I also thought for a minute about how amazed we were when they erected camouflage nets over these immense buildings after Pearl Harbor. From a distance they looked like low hills with roads, trees and small houses, all fake.

Everything was "new" in California, but here, half a world away, everything looked, well, worn out.

Then one car came along with a weak put-put sound as if it was about to die. I recognized it as a 38 or 39 Dodge four door sedan but with a right hand drive. A round metal tank was sticking up out of a hole cut in the trunk lid and a chimney pipe at the top. Small puffs of smoke escaped from under the small tin coolie hat perched atop of the pipe. I stared as it passed by. What the hell was that?

Other sites were there to be seen. A small restaurant with a sign out front; STEAK AND EGGS, 8 Sh's. A rack with the Melbourne newspaper. Alongside a smaller rack with a smaller paper displaying headlines, "YANK SAILORS CAUGHT IN SEX RING." Wow! I wonder what

Mule Ship

that's all about? The other papers had headlines about the war.

Being from LA, trying to not look like a tourist was always important and it seemed I was succeeding, passers by gave me hardly a glance. I felt comfortable.

A hail from the other side of the wide street from guys from my ship startled me. It was Jim Nousler, Jack Funk, Jim Cox, our ships Bos'n and Gene Poole, the only one of the ships crew that was in my section at the Catalina Maritime School. They had two girls in tow. I trotted across the street.

"Hey! I'm glad to see you. I thought I was going to have to check out Melbourne by myself." The taller of the two girls smiled.

"Yes do join us." she quickly said. Not bad looking I thought. Rather tight curly light-brown hair, a loose-fitting dull plain dress much like the other women I had seen. Still, nice looking as I said. Of course I immediately tempered that thought, remembering I had been at sea for almost a month.

That was a common subject among the guys at home. How being away from home affected you sometimes. Stories of soldiers and sailors marrying "native girls" were commonplace. Not me, I would never get sucked in like that.

"My name's Pearl and this is Anita." Anita was short, a bit on the chubby side and looked too young I thought. And I wondered who was with who here? They were chattering about going to 'Luna Park' and they were going to catch the 'Tram.' Pearl had positioned herself alongside me as the group continued down the street. I was encouraged.

"What's Luna Park?"

"You know, they have rides and things to do. All Yanks love to go there!" Pearl said in what I thought was a delightful Australian accent. So I was a "Yank" now. I had never thought of myself that way. "Yankees" were from New England as far as I was concerned. I was a Californian but thought better of mentioning this.

Dick Sproul

About then another of those put-putting cars came by. I had to ask. "What's up with those cars?"

"Oh, that's a Jitney, if you need a ride just wave. You know like a taxi. They only charge half a shilling or so, depending on how far you want to go."

"But what about the smoke stack, what's that for?"

"That's what makes them go, she said. We don't have much petrol you know. They run on coal I think."

On coal? Then I remembered, 10th grade Applied Physics class, Mr. Olney, conducted those fascinating experiments. Levers and gears and ice making, and one where he demonstrated how to produce coal gas. He dropped a piece of coal into a small metal paint can, sealed it shut and placed it over a Bunsen burner. After a minute or so he struck a match and put it to a short tube protruding from the can. Poof, a weak blue flame ignited.

These Australians had figured how to run a car on coal gas. I remembered too from reading those Book of Knowledge volumes that Australia had large coal mines.

"I would like to see some kangaroos," I said.

Pearl laughed, "We have plenty of Kangaroos! but they're all in the zoo now. Melbourne is a big city. We could go there later. Here comes the tram, hurry!"

Arriving at Luna Park we all piled off the tram and entered what was, to me, just a carnival. But, perhaps, a bit more permanent than the carnivals I was used to seeing. A lighted sign arched over the entrance and music came from a whirling merry-go-round. It was quite busy, lots of kids. Again, very few men.

Out of nowhere three small boys descended on Pearl and me."Gotta happney Yank? Gotta happney Yank?" the freckle-faced one said, so very rapidly I didn't think I'd heard it right.

"What?"

Again, "Gotta happney Yank?" I turned to Pearl still totally mystified.

Mule Ship

"He's asking for a half-penny," she carefully enunciated. I reached into my pocked and gave him one of the large Australian coins I had got from the Purser. His eyes bugged at the coin.

"Thanks Yank!" and off they ran.

Pearl laughed, "That was a bit more than a half-penny."

I didn't see much I wanted to do, but others took a couple of rides while we sampled some tea and "scones." I considered, or maybe fantasized is a better term, a Ferris Wheel ride with Pearl but didn't see how that would work out if any of the others decided to come along so I just continued to soak up the Australian scene, watching the people enjoying their day at the park.

Out of the crowd two of the sailors from our navy gun crew appeared. "I see you've made contact." obviously referring to the girls with us. "Did you hear about the party?" This got my attention. "Yeah, we know this girl from our last trip and she says her folks will be gone for the weekend. We're going to her house later. That sounded good, maybe I could get Pearl alone for awhile.

"We were headed for the zoo," Pearl interjected. Yeah, I did want to see those kangaroos!

"OK, we'd like to see the zoo too. We can all go together."

As promised there were lots of kangaroos, big and small but few other animals. A couple of Koala bears, some Kookaburra birds in a gage and a few dingos in a large pen. "Since the war they haven't been able to bring in any new animals." Pearl said. "Besides, meat is rationed."

The sun soon set on this warm summer January day and we headed for the party. The party house turned out to be an older Victorian style not unlike my grandparents house back in LA. The neighborhood looked about the same only a bit shabbier. Australians are not big on landscaping I surmised.

Dick Sproul

The navy guys barged right in liked they owned the place. Some party.

There were only three other sailors and one girl sitting at a kitchen table covered with a worn oilcloth. A whisky bottle, some glasses and a Coke bottle were the only things on it. A few dirty dishes in the sink, counters and cabinets in need of paint. No music, no radio. The sailors, all older, probably in their early or mid 20s, greeted us warmly when they saw we had a couple of girls with us.

"How old are you?" one of them said, looking at Anita.

"18" she answered defiantly. We all knew she was lying.

"Who wants a drink?" Pearl and I didn't respond but the others did.

"Is there any more Coca Cola," Pearl asked.

"Look in the fridge." The girl said. All of the sailors seemed to know her and no introductions were offered. I followed Pearl and she retrieved the lone Coke bottle.

"We can share." she whispered. *That was OK with me. How did she know I didn't drink?"*

It wasn't long before the whiskey bottle was two thirds empty. Cox shoved his glass forward indicating he would like another shot.

"Aren't you too young to be drinking?" One of the sailors challenged.

With that Cox raised his small but stocky frame out of his chair, grabbed the bottle and filled his glass to the brim. Before anyone could protest he chug-a-lugged the full glass down.

This won't wind up good. We hadn't had much to eat. Protests from others only brought a "I'll show you guys!." Cox sat down with a defiant look.

Well, to make a long story short, Cox soon got that glassy look and I knew someone had to get him back to the ship. Since Pearl, Jack Funk and I were the only sober ones there I figured it was us. I gave a long look at Pearl. My fantasy was not to be. Not this night and since our ship was leaving in the morning nor any other night. Still, you never know, we did have the return trip home.

"It's time to leave" I said to Cox and took him by the arm. He didn't protest, he was already too far gone. Jack and I got him out the door, down the steps and headed to the corner. Too late I regretfully remembered I had not asked Pearl for a phone number or address.

By some miracle of fate along came a Jitney. The driver was sympathetic and would take us to the docks, just in time it turned out. Everything came up when Cox exited the Jitney at the dock. Paying the Jitney driver a few shillings we steered Cox through the gate and headed for the ship about a hundred yards away. About half way there his knees buckled. With Jacks help I got Cox over my shoulder. He wasn't as heavy as I expected, still getting up the gangway was a real chore. I had to be careful not to drop him.

Either the dock or the deck would be a tough place to land. That tough football conditioning a few months earlier paid off. Again with Jacks help we poured Cox into his bunk.

I contemplated trying to get back to the party, and Pearl, but I wasn't even sure where the house was. Oh well, probably for the best. Most likely I'll never see her again----

In the morning I again rushed or postponed my duties so I could watch our departure from the boat deck. I knew it would be the best show before the long boring trip to India. One of the Armed Guard sailors was posted at the gangway to secure the ship. A commotion just below me diverted my attention. It was Leonard, the 2nd Cook with his sea bag over his shoulder was headed down the gangway.

"Halt" the sailor commanded. "No one leaves the ship!" Leonard didn't look back. "Halt" the sailor shouted again placing his hand on the 45 strapped to his hip. Leonard kept going, never looking back. By now he was on the dock and rapidly increasing the distance. The sailor shouting in frustration got the attention of the captain and the Armed Guard lieutenant on the bridge. Looking uncertain the captain finally said "Let him go." Leonard was already out of sight anyway.

The crew secured the ladder and with the Mates commands shouted forward and aft it was a repeat of the routine 30 days earlier.

We were soon on our way out of the harbor headed for Calcutta and I was left wondering what that was all about. How could Leonard just walk away? None of the crew had a clue. Asking the captain was out of the question. Oh well, it was not my problem, the authorities will handle it---- wont they? Did Leonard know something we didn't?

The coast off our starboard side soon disappeared. After awhile land could be seen off to the port side to the south. "Tasmania" somebody announced but was immediately corrected by one of the navy gun crew.

"No, that's just a small island, Tasmania is far over the horizon, maybe a hundred miles or more."

Four days of plowing westward the sea getting rougher, not from weather I was told, but the confluence of the currents from the Pacific and Indian Oceans. Monstrous swells rolled the ship making all chores awkward, still no one got seasick. We were in what is called the Australian Bight. That huge "bite" in the southern coast of Australia.

Part II

Scuttlebutt

"Sir, I think I just saw a submarine!"

Army Capt. Hatfield, one of four army officers aboard, looked at the soldier skeptically.

"You think you saw a sub? What's your name private? How come you don't have your shirt on?"

"Pfc. Anderson Sir. It's pretty hot sir and everyone is just wearing T-shirts."

"What did it look like?"

"I was looking at the horizon to see if I could see Australia and just for a moment I saw what looked like a periscope and a conning tower."

Hatfield was skeptical. He hated it when this kind of thing happened. Making it even more difficult was that he was just a passenger on this ship, not the Captain of it. The Officer also knew that the ship was probably hundreds of miles from Australia and now in the Indian Ocean, although he didn't know exactly where. This GI was just being foolish trying to see any land.

"Well, I guess we'll have to tell somebody and next time you come up on the boat deck wear your shirt."

"Yes sir."

Turning, Hatfield strode towards the bridge, the Pfc. following behind him.

Dick Sproul

Poking his head into the open doorway he spotted the Merchant Marine Officer on duty.

"Hi, Excuse me, I have a soldier here who thinks he saw a submarine."

"What? Can I talk to him?"

"Yes sir, he's right here. "Anderson tell the Mate what you saw."

"Yes sir, I was looking off to the right, excuse me sir, the starboard side, and way off there was the top of a sub. You know like just the upper part of a conning tower. That's what it looked like."

"You're sure?"

"Yes sir, I sure saw something."

"Stand by, I'll get Captain Dennis"

He turned to the seaman on standby watch. "Larson, go knock on the Captain's door and ask him to come on to the bridge."

"Yes sir."

In a moment the ship's Captain, looking a bit sleepy after standing on the bridge most of the night entered the wheelhouse. Captain Dennis had made this run twice before and he was really getting tired of it. He considered it a "milk run" well out of the way of any enemy action. Hauling US Army mules to India was not that appealing either. "What's up?"

"Captain we have a soldier here that thinks he saw a submarine". There was only one GI standing there so Dennis addressed him directly. "What did you see soldier?" Anderson repeated what he had told his Captain.

Upon reporting in at Melbourne, the last port of call, Captain Dennis had been informed of recent enemy submarine activity around Melbourne and off the east coast of Australia. The local Commandant suspected it was a single Jap sub that so far had avoided detection. The last report was almost two weeks earlier, which was several weeks after the first and his feeling was that the sub had returned for re-supply or more likely had run into difficulty of its own. The military intelligence noted that the few remaining Japanese subs in the Pacific were practically suicide missions what with lack of spare parts and trained personnel. Now here in the middle of the Indian Ocean 700 hundred miles from the coast of Western Australia he felt far from enemy activity. It had to be impossible for this GI to have seen what he thinks he saw.

"OK soldier, We'll see to it."

Anderson, the son of a lawyer in San Francisco and headed for college when he got out of the army, felt uneasy with the ship Captain's somewhat relaxed response. The Private had been drafted four months earlier and had seen plenty of apathy now that the war was nearly won. His Captain however seeing his hesitation cupped him under the elbow and led him off the bridge.

"You don't need to tell anyone about this. We don't want to get everybody worried."

He knew however that it was unlikely that Anderson would keep this to himself.

What Captain Dennis did not know, and could not know, was that the sub Anderson did see was not actively looking for any ships in these waters. It was simply on it's way to it's home base, the Japanese held port of Singapore.

Its course, over 700 hundred miles off the coast to avoid air patrols. They had some success around Melbourne and Sydney but no way to confirm whether their targets were sunk or just damaged. The crew was tired and several were sick. Supplies were running low. They had three torpedoes left, two of which did not completely check out and their operation doubtful. What Captain Dennis also did not know was that this enemy sub was not a Japanese sub.

> *If you don't think about catastrophe ahead of time, when it happens you won't have any idea how to deal with it]*

Dick Sproul

February 6th, 1945

Eight days out of Melbourne and on course for Calcutta. It's summer down-under in the southern hemisphere and so like most everyone else I'm wearing issue denims with a tee-shirt and the same rough leather boots they issued me at the Maritime School boot camp on Catalina Island. Now on a north-westerly heading, we have officially entered the Indian Ocean. I decide that this night I will go to bed a little earlier. It's been tough getting up so early each morning to start my duties.

      The watch shakes me awake at 6:30 a.m. and each time I swear I'll get to bed earlier. I'm supposed to have quarters made up for the deck officer and the engine room officer coming off the 4 to 8 watch, as well as the Captains quarters. How did I get this crummy job? I should be pulling duty in the Engine room. Even though it's a tougher job, that's what I'm good at. I'm an experienced machinist and overhauled my Ford's engine last summer.

      Captain Dennis always has breakfast before the watch is changed and so this is the only clear time to complete that part of my duties. It's considered good form to take my breakfast after the just-relieved watch has had theirs. Often this means wilted toast or dried out pancakes. Fortunately, eggs are still cooked to order. One of the perks of being in the Merchant Marine.

      Our dinner was good, mutton steaks, (loaded in Australia no doubt) mashed potatoes and a vegetable. Chocolate cake for desert. The Unions have insisted on maintaining peacetime crew conditions, even in wartime. That includes a room steward for ships officers. That's me.

Mule Ship

Four days earlier the 2nd Engineer suffered an acute appendicitis attack. We were in the middle of the Australian Bight, eight hours from Adelaide. Huge swells created by opposing currents from the Pacific and Indian Oceans were making the ship roll 20 degrees or more. The Engineer was given the choice of having the US Army doctor aboard to operate, or wait and be hospitalized in Adelaide. The doctor had no way of knowing how long it would take to get the Engineer to the hospital after we docked or what it would take to set it all up. We couldn't even break radio silence to alert the Aussies that we were coming. Considering the risk of a burst appendix the engineer made the decision to be operated on aboard the ship. Captain Dennis ordered the ship to heave-to into the swell to minimize the roll. Maintaining just enough screw turns to keep our heading. The downside was the fore and aft pitching was almost as bad as the roll. The bow would rise up on the swell and then drop down as it passed under us. The stern then pitched up exposing the screw, subjecting the ship to a worrisome vibration.

The doctor ordered the Army mess table cleared and covered with a mattress and clean sheets that I supplied from the ship's laundry. The Engineer was laid out on the table and strapped down. With a medic and a volunteer to assist, the operation was performed with two GI's each, holding the team's belts to keep them from slipping on the tilting deck. Four hours later, the operation apparently successful and the ship back on course, the Engineer was carried up the steep ladder out of the Army quarters in the ship's hold and put to bed in his own quarters on the boat deck.

Now, as it turned out, a critical four hours behind, we have traveled several hundred miles west and then changed to a northerly heading, staying well clear of the southern tip of Western Australia.

The nearly non-stop card game is going in the mess room with the nightly bull session complementing the ship's social action. Except for those on watch most of the ships crew and some of the navy gun crew are there.

This night I'm successful in tearing myself away. My new waterproof wrist watch says its 9:30. A little earlier I had looked out and there was still a bit of light in the sky. The Head is down the passageway towards my quarters. I don't want to be awakened during the night by a full bladder.

Closing the door of that small steel cubicle I unbutton my fly.

Somehow I knew instantly what the sound meant. It wasn't at all like in the movies. More like some gigantic Paul Bunyon with a huge hammer, the sharp deafening crack seemed to explode off the bulkhead next to my ear. At the same Instant the lights went out. Total darkness. Then, in the time interval it takes a submarine commander to say "fire two!", there was another one, somehow even louder. Thoughts rippled, one over the other, the kick-out panel in the door, get to my foc'sle and life jacket, how much time do I have?

Close to panic, I flung open the door and feeling my way I charged down the passageway to my room. Pounding footsteps echoed down the completely dark passageway. Strangely, I don't remember hearing any voices. Only my heart pounding in my ears.

Stories of Liberty Ships breaking in half and sinking in minutes numbed my brain. I had to force myself to function. In the darkness, I found my life vest right where I always left it, hanging on the end of my bunk, I slipped one arm into it and flipped it around to get the other arm. I sensed my mates in the room with me scrambling for their jackets. Something or someone caught the vest. I swore loudly and jerked the vest free. Easy now, don't panic, the thought quickly replaced by---panic. Gaining the other arm I found my emergency kit under the bed. Precious seconds had slipped by. I would need my P-coat in my locker. I thought about my school letterman sweater, my prized possession, also in the locker. Instead I bolted out without taking either one and up the ladder to the boat deck. Total darkness, the twilight gone. A vague outline of the ships structure and masts is all I can see. Racing across the deck to my lifeboat station on the starboard side, I fall face down on the deck, my arms protecting me. In the darkness I had tripped on potato crates loaded on the boat deck. I could feel the wooden slats.

The crates had broken free and were strewn in my path. Gaining my feet I looked aft. There were two small lights rapidly receding in our wake. Life jacket lights! "My God!" Raising my knees high I scrambled over the debris. No more than two or three seconds later I was at my boat station.

Adjusting a little to the darkness I could see that I was alone. How could I be the first one here? The ship was moving along just as it always has. The white wake running straight out. The two tiny lights no longer visible. Is this some kind of weird, realistic nightmare? I knew it wasn't. The GI's had been ordered to wear their life jackets at all times when on deck. Did they fall? Or did they jump? How would we ever get back to them?

Strangely, water was pouring off of the flying bridge out of the scupper hole in the deck coping. Each time the ship rolled to starboard more water came out. Salt water. I could smell and taste the spray as it poured directly into the number one lifeboat, still secure in its chocks. It was nearly full. The edges of the canvas boat cover protruded out from the water, obviously not properly lashed in place. Then one, then two more and finally the deck was filled with dark forms just standing there, directionless. Less than a minute had passed. Why aren't they doing something, like preparing to lower the lifeboats? I could just make out one of the deck crew. It was Jack Funk. He was wearing his gray chief's hat that Catalina Island Maritime School "graduates", including myself, thought were more "military". I finally took it upon myself.

"Let's get the boat cranked out." I said to Jack.

"OK" he responded.

Adjusting more to the darkness I found the stowed crank handle. I pulled it lose and tried to fit it onto the shaft. The square hole in the handle was supposed to mate with the davit worm drive. It didn't. I couldn't believe it. I tried again and still again. Nothing. Eyes now getting adjusted to the darkness I could see that I had it properly aligned. Someone was holding a battle lantern. I took it and flicked the switch.

"Turn out that light, were still blacked out." came from somewhere. Under the circumstances it seemed an absurd command but I had seen what I needed to.

I turned to Jack. "The damn thing doesn't fit!".

"Yeah, I heard there was a problem with one of the handles"

"You mean they knew about this and no one fixed it? Is this the only one?"

"I think so. We'll just have to wait until we can use a handle from the other boat".

Somewhere between disgust and lessening panic I stood up, eyes now adjusting to the darkness, I pushed through the crowd now gathered around the boats and made my way back to boat number three. Hell, I was in the Stewards Department, where was the rest of the deck crew? They are supposed to take care of this kind of shit!

Did our Captain know about this? Good God! Don't people pay attention! How can people be so oblivious! It could make the difference between getting off this ship alive.

By now boat number three was nearly at the outboard position. Several men already seated in it waiting for it to be lowered. "Hurry, I need that handle, ours doesn't fit",

With a dull thunk, the boat davit hit the outboard stop. The dark figure stood up and backed away, leaving the handle in place. In the darkness he probably couldn't see my glare. I shouldered him aside. I didn't try to see who it was. Squatting, I wiggled the handle free.

Just then, with a deafening, hissing roar the boiler safety valves let go.

A narrow white iridescent column of steam jetted straight up out of the stack. The engine room watch had not turned off the boiler fires. In the darkness it seemed luminescent. A gleaming plume that would be visible for miles.

So much for our blackout. The ship was slowing, nearly stopped now. We had moved a couple of miles or more since I saw the two lights.

With our boat now off it's chocks and out over the water we still had the problem of the water in the boat. Now brim full. With all that water the boat must have weighed tons. I couldn't tell if the automatic drain valve was letting any of the water out. It was still too dark. I remembered that there was a cap that was supposed to be off so that rainwater would drain.

With all the other screw-ups it was probably still in place. Over the roar of the safety valves I yelled "Jack, lets see if the drain valve cap is off. I can't see any water coming out", although in the darkness I couldn't be sure.

We climbed into the boat, water above our knees. I would regret that action. I guess Jack would too. Reaching down, shoulder deep into the water I couldn't identify anything. Was there more than one? Was it in the center? Or nearer the bow or stern? I couldn't remember.

Suddenly it didn't matter. I was weightless, falling. Mental flashes of light, images, faces I think, even though my eyes were tightly closed. My knees instinctively came up, my body into a tuck, arms up over my head.

Plunging into the inky sea my lifejacket brought me, gasping, back to the surface. The lifeboat was swinging wildly by one end, the steel bow passing just inches from my head. Jack was a yard or two away. He retrieved his hat floating next to him and calmly placed it on his head.

"What the hell happened?" He didn't respond. The roar of the safety valves, now supplanted with the water slapping against the ship's hull, was all I could hear.

Although now completely stopped, the ship seemed to be drifting toward us.

Would I be pulled under? The water was oily, I could taste it. The smell was strong. The ships oil bunkers had been breached. The hull, just inches away from my face, is like a monstrous mountain cliff, swaying, rolling, and threatening us. Rust and barnacles rushed by as the six-foot swells elevatored us up and down. Getting sandpapered by that surface would not be good. Were there sharks in these waters?

"Get back" I yelled and with strong backstrokes I tried to move away. My efforts at first were ineffective. We were still inches away from those threatening, rough steel plates that was the *S. S. Peter Silvester*. I could feel oily, slimy ropes in the water. Painter lines meant to be attached to the lifeboat bow to assist when launching under way. Our situation then reversed itself. The gap between the ship and us now quickly widened. Perhaps the ship has slowly rotated and the wind is now pushing it away from us. Not good. Even though we were now only eight or ten yards away I thought of those two small lights now miles behind us.

"Jack we've got to get back on the ship!" A prayer passed quickly through my mind. Now stroking desperately toward the ship, Jack trailing behind me.

Again it seemed as if my efforts were wasted, the bulky lifejacket resisting movement. Then one of the greasy oil-covered lines appeared and I lunged for it. It evaded me. Then I lunged again. I got it! But it was so slippery that I couldn't grip it enough to move myself. Fashioning a small loop in the line I was able to secure a grip and move a bit toward my goal.

Mule Ship

Repeating the action I moved a yard or so closer. And again. A little closer. Several minutes of that and I was there!

I've got to get back on deck! I strained to see if the chain ladder had been lowered down the side of the ship. It wasn't really a ladder. More of a net-like affair eight or nine feet wide made of chain fashioned into foot wide squares. Normally rolled and stowed between the lifeboat and the gun whale or "gunnel", its purpose to allow several men at a time to climb down into the lowered life boat. It was either not there or it was too dark. Minutes passed and I prayed.

Somehow the lifeboat had now been returned to it's level position. The bottom of the boat partly blocking my view of the deck and of course also blocking the view of those on the deck. I Screamed "lower the net!" as loud as I could. I whistled and yelled, again and again, but the roaring steam from the safety valves swept my voice away. In desperation I turned the lens of my life jacket light, this pushed the base of the bulb down onto the battery terminal. Rotating the lens back turned it off. On off, on off. I pulled myself even closer. The rust and barnacles were again right in my face. There it was! Now I could see it! I stretched up as far as I could, the end of the ladder was still out of reach. The line I was grasping was of no use, it lead off at an angle toward the bow. Kicking frantically I made another try. I fell back, oily water filling my nose. I've got to do this!

Immediately, inexplicitly, like a great watery cradle, an ocean swell, larger than the others, lifted me. High enough for my foot to land on the bottom chain. My hands a couple of squares above that. I was like a fly on the wall. I took a step or two up.

Where was Jack? Looking back I could see him seemingly making little effort to come in my direction. "Come on Jack, this way!". If he got close I could reach down and help him. My voice, again washed away by the roar of the jetting steam. I almost let go. But would I get another chance? Could I get back up one more time? I

Dick Sproul

shouted again and this time waved him on. Did he respond? I couldn't be sure. It was just too dark to be sure. But how could he not see me? By now he was about fifteen feet out and moving towards the now settling bow. It was clear that the torpedo hits were having some effect, but I was now beginning to doubt that this sturdy ship was going to sink.

Maybe Jack figured that he would have better chance getting on deck at the bow. Or maybe he didn't want to get back on a sinking ship. But somehow I knew that my action was right. I should go back and get him. I just couldn't let go. My fingers were frozen to the chain. Another regret.

Regaining the deck I looked around to find the 2nd mate. He was supposed to be in charge of my boat station. I was soaked, feeling the chill and thinking about my P-coat still in my locker. Leaving the boat deck and going back down into the ship was an action I was reluctant to take. If the ship suddenly started to sink I might be trapped. That vision terrified me. A figure appeared up on the flying bridge, it was the captain. "Don't lower those boats till I tell you to!" he hollered. "We can save her!" I looked again towards the bow.

Even in the darkness I could make out that the bow was getting very low in the water. I could now see that several of the people on the deck were GIs up from their quarters in the hold. One was propped up against the bulkhead, injured. Most of them I could see had no life jackets. I remembered that there was a pile of old cork jackets lashed on the flying bridge. No doubt left over from an earlier voyage before the newer kapok jackets were issued. Locating the ladder I climbed up. Of the four gun tubs with their 20 mm guns only one was manned. It was Joe Crete, one of the navy gun crew.

"Are you the only one here, where are the others?" I couldn't believe it.

"I don't know, I haven't seen anybody." he said.

Mule Ship

I didn't say anything, but what was going on? The Captain was just up here. I found the lifejackets and released the half hitch from the cleat. Leaning over the rail I yelled down to the boat deck. It was too dark to see if anyone was standing below my position. There was no response. Reaching down as far as I could I dropped each jacket. They disappeared into the darkness. Even though the jackets were not heavy the solid cork dropping on someone' head might be unpleasant but I couldn't worry about that. It was more important that those without jackets have them. I turned to Crete, "Do you need any help? Are your spare magazines cranked up?"

"I haven't had a chance to do that"

Each gun tub had two lockers with four magazines each loaded with fifty rounds of 20-mm ammunition. Four magazines would have their feeding springs cranked and four would be relaxed. One of the ready magazines would be mounted on the gun, the others remaining in the locker. Opening the ammo locker I found the crank handle and quickly applied the spring tension to each magazine. Somehow there was just enough starlight filtering through the clouds to do this.

"OK, we're all set now."

"Thanks, I sure appreciate this" His remark seemed odd under the circumstances, as though his role as an Armed Guard meant that he was my protector. After all, my ass was on the line too.

"Hey, it's what we're supposed to do. But where is everyone" I repeated.

"I was down in the hold" he said. "With the GI's. Some of the guys were on the hatch playing cards. It went up and then came down. They just disappeared! It got dark and there was a lot of smoke and at first I couldn't see anything. Then I could see the sky where the hatch had been.

Dick Sproul

It took me awhile to get out. I just got up here before you came"

I could imagine what happened to the card players and why the other gun tubs were empty. Also the terror that Crete must have felt. We stood there, Crete strapped into the gun harness, ready for anything, doing what he was trained to do.

"Maybe I should ready one of the other guns?" We had been trained on the Swedish designed, 20mm Orlikon gun at the Maritime School on Catalina. Each of the Merchant Marine crew had also fired a few rounds during our only gun exercise crossing the Pacific. I knew how to engage the first round and how to aim and fire the gun. Actually hitting anything was another matter.

Just then the Navy Gunnery Petty Officer came up the ladder. "Secure that gun we are abandoning ship!" Just as quickly he disappeared. What the hell!

Mixed signals here. Crete released one of the shoulder straps and slipped out of the other. We climbed down to the boat deck. Visibility was at times a bit better but the overcast still obscured the stars. Perhaps the moon had risen. I could make out Lt. Burch, one of the Army officers coming up the ladder carrying someone on his shoulder. Burch was a large fellow, an inch or two taller than I and with big shoulders and arms. Rumor was that he was a pro football player before joining the army. He laid his burden gently onto the deck and turned back down the ladder. The noise of the escaping steam from the safety valves that been blotting out other noises suddenly stopped. Perhaps someone had the guts to go down into the engine room and shut off the fires. Or perhaps the boilers had simply run out of steam. It was a welcome silence and our position was no longer marked by that towering column of white steam.

My clothes were starting to dry but I was getting cold and shivering a bit so I again thought about getting my P-

Mule Ship

coat from my locker. That would require me going down into my quarters on the main deck. What if the ship suddenly sank while I was down there? With that vision in mind I quickly rejected the idea. I then remembered the 2nd. Mate's quarters were just off the boat deck on the starboard side. The 2nd Mate was nowhere in sight.

Opening the door and locating his closet I could only find a light sport jacket. Somehow there was enough light. Taking off my lifejacket, if only for a minute, took all the resolve I could muster. That lifejacket had already saved my life once. Immediately warmed by the dry jacket I figured I had better get out of there. He might think I was stealing something. But then the absurdity hit me. Stepping out onto the deck with the others I spotted the Mate. I made my way toward him.

A brilliant flash of light! Muffled, but still a fearful explosion. Water rained down followed by heavy thumps of objects striking the deck. The cover of the flying bridge was ten feet away. Instead I lunged toward the bulkhead and flattened myself against it hoping that anything coming down would be at least be deflected. My back to the bulkhead, I saw something burning in the sky. Sparks were trailing from it. My God! They are shelling us. No, it's a flare! And there, there it was, the submarine! I could see it. On the surface, no more than a half mile off. It's silhouette easily seen. I flinched, anticipating the muzzle blast from the five-inch cannon on our ship's fantail. I remembered how incredibly loud that gun had been during our Pacific practice. It made me jump each time they fired it no matter how much I steeled myself. How could they miss? It would be like shooting fish in a barrel. But there was only silence. The gun was unmanned.

Within seconds the Captain again appeared on the flying bridge. Where had he been? "Lower those boats, abandon ship, abandon ship!" He turned and disappeared.

Dick Sproul

Stepping through seemingly immobile figures between me and the lifeboat, I moved over to the forward bit. Where was the deck crew? I loosened the hitch and a couple of turns of the line. Still holding two turns on the bit I looked to see if the aft falls were manned. I held the line taut. There were people in the way. Then the 2nd. Mate's voice "boat number one, ease off on those lines, lower away!" I gave it some slack letting the weight of the boat overcome the grip of the turns on the bit and the boat started to lower. I let the line pull each hand closer to the bit making sure I had a firm grip with the other hand before letting go. There were already several men in the boat. I made out several old timers from the stewards department.

These were the guys that ridiculed us "Catalina Kids". These were the mess men who served the tables in the officer's mess and the dishwasher and one of the cooks. Their boast that if we ever got torpedoed- "These Catalina kids are gonna be shittin their pants while we lower the boats". And "We'll probably have to carry them".--Yeah, sure.

"Easy aft" the Mate called out, then "slack off forward"

I could see the boat level off as I followed the Mate's directions. The Mate was now visible as the deck cleared of men and starlight or maybe moonlight penetrated the thinning cloud cover. By now the boat was nearly full. But more were coming and climbing down the chain net that I had used earlier. "Slack off fore and aft, lower away". With the mates instructions the boat was dropping evenly. Feeding the line steadily I moved closer to the edge. As the boat touched the water the Mate called "Slack off fore and aft!" I threw off the last two turns and the line went slack. The boat now riding in the water.

There was no room for me. The boat was already overloaded. A figure standing in the bow had loosened the shackle and was holding the block to keep the boat from drifting away. I felt the Mate's hand pulling on my arm. "Get off, get into the boat!". I reached out and grabbed one of the knotted ropes hanging from the cable stretched between the davits and went down hand over hand. I ended up on someone's lap. They squeezed over and somehow made room.

    Some were sitting on the very bottom of the boat. For others there was only room to stand. Looking forward, the water was moving slowly up the ship's deck. A few feet of the bow had completely disappeared. The stern was lifting and I could now see a dim outline of a blade of the ship's propeller. Our boat was still along side, only a foot or two away from the same barnacles and rust I had faced thirty minutes earlier.

    "We've got to get clear" I yelled. Pulling out an oar I stabbed at the side of the ship.

    "Wait, there's still men in the water" someone else shouted as another swimmer was pulled in. I could see 2 or 3 others nearby, their lifejackets keeping their heads well above water. But by now our boat was in danger of being swamped. Only 3 or 4 inches of freeboard separated our gunnels from the water. For a moment the darkness was less so and I could see more of the ship.

    "It's going down" I hollered back "We can't help them if we get pulled under with it." Now pushing the oar as hard as I could, the space widened. Someone else started to push. We moved a bit further away. Now there was room to dip the oars in the water. Two more oars were unlimbered, oarlocks inserted and the gap was widened a yard or two further. The men still in the water were hanging on to the side. We were still too close. The ship was tilting more steeply. We pulled hard.

    All eyes turned toward the ship, we froze, each man suddenly immobile. A terrible scream, louder than any human could ever make, a screeching, rending, crashing sound as one inch steel plates were ripped apart. The entire forward section of the ship disappeared in an explosive roaring, boiling cauldron of foaming sea. The water where we had been, rushed into the vortex.

The bow section with a hundred mules, the forward gun tub, all the ships rigging and the Army enlisted quarters—were any men still in there?-- was gone. The stern section, including the engine room and the "house" with bridge and quarters, now relieved of the tremendous weight of the riddled bow, shot upwards, pivoting on the buoyancy still encased in the intact compartments.

For a split fraction of a second the sheared off end of the ship cleared the water. I thought I could see clear under hull. I had an image of the life boats on the other side. Then it came plunging down sending a wave of water towards us. I pulled on the oar but it would be too late. But perhaps not. The slight turn of the boat put our stern into the wave.

Shipping only a small amount of water over the gunwale the wave split, moving harmlessly past us, .A rebound of the severed ship created another wave, but less intense than the first. We were OK. But were there any men still on that bow section? Where was Jack? We pulled the remaining two men into the boat and miraculously we're not swamped. The other starboard lifeboat was barely visible a few yards away.

It appeared to be swamped, only it's air tanks keeping it afloat. We could see there were only two men still in it. "Are you OK?" was shouted out

"We have an injured man" came the reply. The oars went out to move toward them. The darkness closed in.

"I hear an engine!" It was the man sitting at my feet on the bottom of the boat. I hadn't heard a thing. Almost before his voice died out the sea seemed to rise up not fifty feet away. Seawater cascading down from the conning tower and deck, white foam outlining its shape, the submarine surfaced, its diesel engines throbbing. I strained to see men on its deck. They would have guns. I could only make out the shape of the sub. They are going to strafe us! Should I dive into the water? I knew bullets don't travel very far in water. If I could get deep enough! But with my life jacket on I would not be able to. I reached for the knot. There wasn't time! Perhaps they won't, or perhaps the bullets will miss me, I prayed. Somehow a silly thought blended in. My hair will turn white; there is no way I could be any more frightened than I am now. If anyone ever had his hair turn white from fear then mine must. How could it not? It was impossible for anyone to be more frightened.

It could have been a lifetime; it might have been a minute. Time became unreal, unused here. The drumm - drumm of the subs engines was the only connection to reality.

But the sub moved away from us and disappeared into the darkness. We could hear its engines as the sub circled the area. Then the sound faded away. They didn't come back. We were alone, the other boat had disappeared, the darkness deeper now. Only silence, darkness,

My stomach lurched. I felt it turning inside out. I clawed over the man next to me. "Hey!" Then he moved back. I just managed to get my head over the side of the boat. Belly muscles convulsing, over and over it all came up. Retching again and again even though there was nothing more to give. Why was I so sick? Was it seasickness from the movement of the boat? Why didn't I get sick during the 28 day trip to Melbourne? And then when they slowed the ship to perform the appendectomy on the 3rd Engineer? The huge ocean swells where the Indian Ocean and the Pacific currents met caused severe rolling. Slowing and then turning into the swell was the best tactic to steady the ship for the operation, but still each time the she nosed down into the trough the propeller cleared the water shaking the whole ship.

Dick Sproul

Was it the strong fuel oil smell when Jack and I were dropped into the water? I didn't swallow any, or did I? I do remember the oily taste in my mouth. Oh God! that's what may have happened to Jack. But if he was overcome by fumes then why wasn't I? Why didn't I go back and get him? I could have held my breath that long. Damn, damn!

With the two boats, one afloat, the other occasionally visible and apparently swamped, we sat there our minds dull with shock. It had been an hour, maybe two, the boats gently rising and falling with the swells. A grunt, a rustle of movement as someone tried to get comfortable.

We were suddenly bathed in an incredibly bright light. It came from high up. For an instant I saw a searchlight that could only come from the bridge of a large ship. Rescue! But there was no ship. My mind adjusted. It was the full moon, now seeming incredibly bright as the heavy clouds opened a moment to reveal its full face. The pupils of our eyes now fully dilated making it seem so bright. The clouds closed and darkness surrounded us again.

But perhaps it was a signal, He was saying "I see you guys, just hang in there, I am looking out for you."

Soon things quieted down again. We were safe, for the moment anyway. All of us I'm sure, thinking of what we had just experienced. I had done the things I had been taught at the Maritime school. In spite of the panic, I had performed, I had moved, not just standing there waiting for others to save me. Considerable satisfaction in that! Thanks, Catalina Island instructors. But eventually there would be more to thank. Thanks Mr. Olney, my high school Applied Physics teacher who taught about wheels and pulleys and levers and pressure. Thanks to Dad for showing me how to use tools and to Coach Edelson on how to use my strength and be determined, oh so determined. Most of all thanks right now to God for delivering me from that dark, oily, heaving, choking water.

Dick Sproul

The Morning

My stomach still roiling, sickness still with me, the morning light revealed our situation. Off a half-mile or so was the stern section of our ship, pitching and rolling, but otherwise doing quite well. We wondered about our cargo. What of the Army mules we were to have delivered to Calcutta. Or rather what was left of them. Almost half of them were on the forward section and they were gone. But what about those still in the aft section? The mules were destined for Burma to help transport supplies to the Army fighting the Japanese.

East of us, a mile or more, were the other two lifeboats. A little closer but more to the north I could see two of the ship's four large life rafts loaded with men. Crate-like affairs about ten feet square, they seemed to be pitching rather strongly. The wind had picked up and the sea had become a bit rough. We could imagine how miserable they were. Our companion boat was still swamped; its two occupants had been unable to bail fast enough to get it afloat. They had reported that a third figure lying flat on the seats was dead, his body partly awash.

Among those in our boat was the 2nd radio operator. He reported that no SOS was transmitted because the first torpedoes knocked down the antenna. The portable radio intended to be used in a life boat had been ruined when the port side boats were swamped during their launch: His boat station had been on the port side but he moved over to the starboard side when he saw we had a dry boat.

It was decided that some in our dangerously overloaded boat move into the swamped boat to help bail it out. Four immediately did so. After a few minutes of frantic bailing they managed to remove water faster than it flowed over the gunnels and the boat began to rise out of the water. It was further decided that we should equalize the number of people in each boat. We could see that the other boat was covered with a thick layer of coagulated fuel oil so any more potential volunteers were understandably reluctant. Finally the 2nd Mate, for some reason, suggested the one Engine Room Officer we had aboard choose at random eight more to go over. He picked three or four close to him and then spotted me. He knew me. I was the officer's steward.

"OK, Sproul, You go over".

I was tempted to protest. This was the boat I was assigned to and had helped launch successfully. Without comment I climbed over and tried to scrape away enough of the thick black goo to make a space to sit. Scraping the surface with my pocket knife worked best. Scrape a blade full, wipe with my finger and with a wrist snap fling it into the sea. Repeat. After an hour or so we had cleared most of the flat surfaces.

Dick Sproul

The Real Beginning

So here we are, February 7th 1945, somewhere 150 miles east of Perth, Western Australia, so we were told. We were to discover days later that it was actually 750 miles. No SOS message had been sent and the many men on rafts clearly in need of quick rescue. We were in boats with small sails we could rig and food and water rations for 10 days. A stiff breeze was blowing directly east toward Australia. Sailing day and night we could be there in three, maybe four days at most.

We could set here for days before a ship happened by. The guys on the rafts wouldn't last that long. Most of us had no idea how much ship traffic there would be in this area. A ship would have to pass within ten miles of us to spot us. My thought was that few ships were going to India this late in the war and that we might never be found. Others shared my view, but we had to take care of things now.

The sky gray, overcast, the west wind brisk, perhaps 7 or 8 knots with a six foot swell running at short intervals and an occasional whitecap showing. To the south, perhaps a half a mile or more, the aft part of the ship, it's entire bow section ripped off, was still afloat. Riding rather well it seemed. Rolling somewhat, but otherwise looking in good condition. The exposed engine room bulkhead apparently holding up well. I remembered a news account early in the war of a liberty ship breaking in half during a storm just like our ship has done. Faulty welds were to blame. The crew of that ship was able to restart the engines and nurse it into port.

Mule Ship

Maybe we could do the same thing. And the mules, still alive! What about them?

During the starless night, wedged into the rocking boat, nothing but blackness all around, my stomach still feeling as though it was full of snakes, it got quiet, very quiet. I had thought about home. I imagine every other man did also. I thought about my mother and how she would cry when she got the news. I wonder how long it will take before they report us missing.

We weren't due in Calcutta for another two weeks. If we get picked up right away maybe I can send a telegram letting her know that I am all right. I thought about my dad, and my brother, Gene, who was in Germany in the Army. An MP, he wasn't near the fighting. But hey, supposedly neither was I, and look where I am! Some of those GIs in the hold of the ship probably had told their folks they too weren't in the infantry and would not be close to any danger. I wonder how many did not make it out? What will their folks be told? And what about Jack? God! I should have gone back after him. I've been worried about him ever since he did not show up on the boat deck. He had plenty of time to make it back if he had re-boarded the ship at the bow. But suppose he stayed there for some reason? Why didn't he follow me? I swept away the vision of him still being on the bow when it plunged to the bottom. He must be in one of the other boats. I have to believe that he is.

On the horizon a couple of miles to the west, the other two lifeboats were close together. Somewhere between the ship and the two boats were two of the large life rafts crowded with men. Ocean swells were rocking the rafts quite a bit. Even at that distance it looked like they were having a miserable time. I wonder how many of them are as sick as I am?

Dick Sproul

Our boat, boat number One, was overloaded but not taking any water. The other starboard lifeboat, boat number 3, the only boat with an engine was about 50 yards away, in not such good shape. Totally swamped, only it's sealed air tanks keeping it afloat, two men were sitting on the seats with a third man laying half submerged, his head and shoulders above the water. Boat No. 3 was supposed to be the Captain's boat since it was the only boat with an engine. I wondered what had happened to the Captain.

We opened the equipment lockers and found the compass and unlashed the boat's rudder stowed under a seat. Extending the oars and installing the rudder, we rowed towards the other boat. Even with two men on each oar some had to move out of the way to clear the swing of the oarsmen. We had earlier found the boat's water supply. Sealed half gallon cans, we opened with P-38 can openers that the GIs had attached to their dog tags. A necessary tool for opening K-Rations.

We hailed the other boat and asked how they were doing and if the prone man was badly hurt. "I think he's dead" came the reply.

When we were close enough someone heaved a line and we pulled the two boats together, bow to stern. The other boat was covered with a thick black layer of coagulated fuel oil. The man lying on the seat was covered with the oil, as was the lower half of the other two. I recognized one of the men as the Chief Engineer. The other was one of the Navy armed guards. "Pancho" was his nickname. He had stayed through the night in the swamped boat with the chief and the dying soldier when all the others left for our boat.

The dead fellow was one of the soldiers that were billeted in number 3 hold. Probably a draftee which would make him the same age as me. Still visible under the oil stains, the olive colored T shirt and dungarees. Maybe he was the one I saw Lieutenant Burch carrying. The top part of the olive drab tee shirt wasn't too badly stained, unlike the GI fatigue pants which were thickly coated. With laced-up boots on his feet, I pictured him playing cards on the hatch cover when it went up with the blast.

With me in boat No. 3 were several people that I was familiar with. The Second Engineer, the Second Mate and the Chief Steward, Louis Defore, were the only ship's officers aboard. Gene Poole who was with me at the Catalina Maritime school. The other Merchant Seamen aboard I only knew by a single name. There was Cox, the designated Bosn's Mate, and Kent, Noussler and Larson. Like me, they too were first-timers from the Maritime training school on Catalina Island.

The 2nd Radio Operator was also among the group and said that no message went out because the radio antenna had come down when the first torpedoes hit. He also said that the portable emergency radio had apparently not worked either. Probably because it got wet. He said the boats on the other side had been improperly launched and were swamped just like boat number three. I wondered about this very crucial statement when I remembered that his boat station should have been on the port side where the radio shack was. I asked him about that. He said that when he saw the portside boats were swamped he hurried over to the starboard side and saw that we had launched a dry boat. So much for boat station drills. That explained why we were so overloaded.

The first order of business was to get the Boat No. 3 bailed out. Since I was in the boat assigned to me during emergency drills I felt that those who had left the swamped boat should be the ones to go back to it. And three or four did get up and climb over taking a bucket and a couple of empty water cans to help with the effort.

At first their frantic bailing seemed of no avail but then gradually the water was thrown out faster than it flowed

Dick Sproul

back over the gunwales, often called "gunnels" and the boat began to rise. Once the gunnels were clear the process became more efficient and the boat quickly became seaworthy. The next seemingly impossible task was to scrape off the thick, dark oil coating. It was then that someone made the comment that we were still overloaded and that some additional transfer should be made. No one else volunteered.

The second mate, the most senior deck officer, for some reason selected the second engineer to pick at random a few more to go over. He immediately pointed to three or four others and they stood up and moved towards the other boat. Then his eyes fell on me. He knew me.

"Sproul, you too" he said.

I was tempted to protest leaving my nice clean boat for a seat in that black goop. I had, after all, handled the forward falls and felt somewhat proud that we had launched our boat successfully. I had already been in the water and had a bit of oil smell in my clothes. But of course I realized that I could not object. I moved over to the other boat and after futilely trying to scrape a place clear with my fingers, finally used my handkerchief. Still a bit of the dark slimy ooze remained on the seat.

When there were 15 of us in the boat plus the dead soldier, it was decided that considering the space taken up by the engine we were about even. That left 22 men in boat No. 1. We also divided up the extra water cans that had been dropped into the bottom of boat No. 3. I wonder who had the good sense to do that?

The gun crew sailor nick-named Pancho tells of mules trying to climb up onto the swamped boat and he alone beating them off with an oar. *This guy ought to get a medal.*

We opened the containers that were fixed adjacent to the benches in mid boat and discovered our supplies and equipment. These boxes were constructed of heavily galvanized steel about a foot and a half square and two and a half feet deep. Each had a lid secured with a dozen or more wing nuts. And of course these tanks also contributed to the floatation when the boat was swamped. There was a tool kit with a hammer, pliers, screwdriver and a small Crescent wrench. The remaining space was filled with food rations. The compass box was also brought out. Within the box was a finely crafted instrument about five inches in diameter, gimbal mounted and liquid filled. And there was a hatchet stowed at each end of the boat placed there in the event that the falls could not be released the rope could be chopped away. The metal cover over the engine, smooth and flat, also made a good seat as did the 40 gallon fuel tank. There was no fishing kit.

    We all continued to scrape away at the oil covered surfaces using knife blades, our bare hands and handkerchiefs. Of course once the handkerchiefs were soiled there was no way to clean them. Dipping them into the salt water did not help. We wrung them out and shoved them back into our pockets. With care the knife blades worked the best. This required wiping the blade with your fingers and then with a snap of the wrist flinging the wad of goop into the sea. By now pant legs were covered with oil. Over the next days the denim fabric would become stiff as the oil dried.

    Next we set about stepping the mast that was lashed to the seats. This was a task that we had practiced on Catalina Island. About eight inches in diameter at its base and maybe twelve feet high and supported with guy wires it appeared very sturdy. Instead of breaking out the sails we concentrated on getting the engine started. With the engine running we could round up the other boats and get the rafts tethered together. Maybe there's room in the boats to take some of the guys off of the rafts.

Dick Sproul

I checked out the engine controls and opened the fuel tank. It was full, gasoline right to the top. Or so it appeared. There was a simple rope pull similar to an out board motor to start the engine. Switch on and fuel valve opened, I wrapped the rope around the pulley and gave a pull. Nothing. A second and third try and still nothing. After several more tries the engine just sputtered and then died. I kept trying, over and over again. Already feeling weak and still nauseous I did not want to give up. Every sputter teased us to try again

Cox offered that when they tested it each week the engine caught usually after two or three pulls and ran very well. Others took over until they were exhausted too.

"Maybe there's water in the magneto" I suggested. "Get me the screwdriver out of the tool kit and I'll open it up". I had learned a little about magnetos in shop class at Fremont High School. We pulled the cover off of the engine and set to work. The magneto was dry, the gaskets had done their job. Then I went to work on the carburetor. The fuel line poured clear but there might have been some water mixed with gas in the carburetor. That was to be expected. I dried it out as best I could and re-assembled every thing.

We tried again, this time pulling off one of the plug wires to check for spark. Aggravated with myself, because I should have done this first. A crisp blue spark snapped across the gap. I've got to think! I know engines, what am I missing?

"Magneto's OK so why won't it start?" We kept trying and again got a sputter or two. My first thought was that there may be a problem with the fuel pump until I realized that the carburetor was down low and was gravity fed. There was no fuel pump!

After awhile, my strength ebbing, we gave up and set the sail hoping that we could get back to the ship and maybe get the radio working. This turned out to be frustrating for me and also crucial in limiting our success. The as yet unforeseen ordeal may have been avoided.

Mule Ship

Considering the time we had spent trying to get the engine to run I was puzzled as to why the other boats on the horizon had not hoisted their sails and tried to join with the rafts or with us. We were downwind from them and reaching us would have been easy with the wind coming directly out of the West. They could also have returned to the ship which was now Southeast from their position.

We tried rowing towards the ship for a couple of hours. If we could just get back aboard and maybe get some fresh fuel or somehow get the radio to work. It was hard work, the boat was heavy and even though I could see our movement through the water the *Peter Silvester* seemed to get no closer. Exhausted, we finally gave up. It was as though the wind was pushing the Silvester away as fast as we were rowing.

There were three sails carefully folded into the sail bag. All dyed a bright red, a mainsail, a jib and a heavy canvas storm jib made up the collection. The "Catalina Kids" aboard had all been through the Maritime School sailing instruction so stepping the sturdy mast and rigging the sails was quickly completed. I did not mention my experience sailing small boats off Newport Harbor with my brother. My mistake. Not that anyone would have understood but that experience made me aware of wind and sail angles and keel pressures. Yet to understand was how important that lifeboats have no keel.

After more hours of slowly sailing across the west wind we seemed to be going more west than south and the gap to the ship undiminished.

The first day ended. Darkness closed us in and we wondered if the ship, the rafts and other boats would be there in the morning. We lowered the sails and began our second long night feeling the ocean swells beneath our boat.

Dick Sproul

Newport Harbor--"Balboa"

*B*alboa--was the name we used because the popular Balboa Island that dominated the harbor, had become the busy destination for anyone wanting to vicariously experience the life of the rich. A pavilion and small beach and pier on the peninsula side of the channel where sail boats could be rented made it possible for most anyone to live the "good life" for an afternoon. Our wonderful Aunt Ruth would drive us and sometimes provide the dollar for the hour rental. A ten and twelve year old had a fine time on these Saturday or Sunday afternoons. Gene and I had learned a lot about sailing during those summer visits.

    Gene of course had picked the brain of the rental operator---got all the do's and don'ts; "Never turn downwind, you will get smacked with the boom. Secure the mainsail line with only one turn on the cleat and if a gust starts to capsize the boat you can release sail pressure and right the boat." He added one more thing. "Boats under sail have the right-of-way over power boats." Yeah, we soon learned that the power boats could care less! They would come boring down the channel throttles set, course set, and would yell furiously, or honk their horn if they had to change course or throttle back when the wind died and we found ourselves caught in their path. Keeping well out of their path seemed like the best thing, only cutting across the channel when the wind was up. Not <u>always</u> possible.

    Of course it wasn't long before we saw other rental boats, flat on their sides, people in the water, the rental launch racing out to the rescue.

Mule Ship

How could they be so stupid? That was the fun of sailing, tacking into the wind, boat heeled over, balancing sail and rudder to get the most speed. To let the boat go on over--well--you just weren't paying attention. Sometimes we did have to be quick if a sudden gust hit.

Cushions stashed under the seat were labeled "Can Be Used for Floatation in Emergencies," ha! We could swim! The little Cat Boats we first rented had a retractable keel. Just a flat board inside a well in the center of the boat and adjustable with a rope for retracting the keel if you wanted to run up it up on the beach.

What would happen if we pulled up the keel while sailing?

Out in the middle of the bay we tested this. Sailing along we found that we couldn't raise it, the side pressure prevented it. OK, we lowered the sail and the keel came up easily. The function of a keel we now fully understood. Further testing with the keel pulled up the boat seemed to sail quite nicely. However, the wake trailed off at an angle. The boat would go sideways as much as forward. Sometimes more! The keel was essential to getting to where you wanted to go.

A little older and with some of our own money we decided to rent a larger sloop. Two dollars an hour! These 14 foot boats could hold six people and with a jib rigged and large main it would really move! A small plaque warned "Do not leave the harbor with this boat." We faithfully observed this rule,--until the day we didn't.

It was truly a beautiful day. Blue skies, a cloud here and there, a brisk wind, perfect sailing weather! We were at the south end of the bay, the wide channel leading out to the ocean in front of us. Wonder what it's like out there? We had taken a trip on the SS Catalina, again with our Aunt Ruth and there were sailboats like the one we were in, out there in the Catalina channel, miles from land.

"Let's do it!" We headed out. The open sea!

Dick Sproul

Clearing the breakwater two foot swells soon became six foot swells, thankfully no whitecaps. Down in the trough only the wide cloud-free sky was visible, while rising to the top we could see everything. Thrilling, which means we were a little scared and therefore very cautious at first. Bravery returning, we tightened the main and the jib. We picked up speed, Wow!

Hanging on to the main and jib lines we leaned out over the windward side trying to counter-balance the pressure on the sail. We were really sailing! Bow spray stinging our faces, frothy wake behind us, up over the swell, zooming down the lee side, we were sailing!

But our hour was up and we had to go back. Coming about—real sailor talk now--we hurried back.

And now here I am in a boat not much larger, with a main sail and a jib but a long way from Newport Harbor. Someone suggested that we ought to know everyone's name. Most of the ships crew knew who the Chief Engineer was but he seemed to be in shock and non-communicative. Actually, it was just that he was quite deaf and had lost his hearing aid. We learned later that he had been off watch and in the sack when the torpedoes hit and was not able to find his teeth either. This small, toothless, shriveled up man had gone down to the sea as a young boy in the 1890's, served in the World War, now called WW I, and was here in still another war, twenty-five years later. Looking very old, very frail, probably in his 60s, but looking 80. All of those years in the engine room, listening to the roar of the boilers, the pounding and clanking of ships engines, had reduced his hearing to the point where we had to yell to make him understand.

We rigged the bow spray curtain, a bright yellow hood-like affair that would keep water out of the boat if we hit heavy seas. Curved steel rods supported and gave it shape making a perfect shelter for the Chief. There were two woolen blankets with the rest of the boat's gear. Wrapping one blanket over his shoulders and the other around his legs we had him move into what was now a snug little home.

Of course at the time we did not think of it that way then but that's what it was to become.

Louis Defore, the pudgy Ship's Purser and Chief Steward, introduced himself to those who might not have known him. The four army people of our newly formed crew being the only ones who were not part of the usual night gatherings in the ship's mess.

Vito Carubo, tall, lanky with tightly curled black hair, the only other member of the "black gang" besides the Chief Engineer, introduced himself. Carl Phieffer, quiet, good sized fellow wearing the traditional white (now dirty) cap I had seen at the Union Hall and the other member of the Stewards Department was next. These three all looked to be in their thirties. Phieffer was probably the oldest. Jim Nossler, Jack Cox, Ken Penn and Jack Larson, all members of the ship's deck crew and, like myself, "Catalina Kids", were next to speak up.

"Dick Sproul, Steward's Department", I couldn't bring myself to say "Bedroom Steward."

Then the Army Lieutenant James Eiselstien was next and I couldn't help but notice the slight emphasis he placed on the "Lieutenant". He was proud of that rank. He too was about 30 or maybe 35 years old. Then, Michael Martinelli, Chuck Kemmer and Tom Tschirhart, all Privates in the Army. Caselli and Capello, who surprisingly, called each other "Pancho" and "Ginea", were the only two from the Navy gun crew. Young guys, probably still in their teens. That completed the roster. Fifteen in all.

The next day passed and no sign of rescue. The line we had attached between the two boats would keep us together during the night. Another long night. The first of many it turned out. Next morning the ship, or what was left of it, had drifted even farther away. The other two boats also seemed farther off on the western horizon. The rafts now almost invisible. Why hadn't the other boats joined up with the rafts? Or why hadn't they tried to get back to the ship? It was downwind from them! Nether boat had even stepped the mast or rigged any sail.

Even with my limited experience sailing small boats I knew that with a ten knot wind out of the west a properly trimmed sail boat can easily make six knots. Averaging only three or four knots this blunt-ended life boat could cross the 150 miles in three days, sailing day and night, maybe four, maybe five, at most. Those guys on the rafts wouldn't last more than a week or two. With no SOS transmitted and just depending on the small chance of a ship coming by, setting sail and getting to Australia sure seemed the right thing to do. With absolute confidence we hoist the sails and begin our journey. Boat number one and boat number three will get to Australia and give the alarm.

Mule Ship

Part III
The Decision

*W*e were eager to get going.---I was eager to get going.---Just sitting here and hoping that some ship would pass close enough to spot us did not seem to be wise. There might never be a ship that would come close enough. We had not seen a single ship since leaving Melbourne. In a small boat, the horizon is only five or six miles away. To think that a ship would pass within a circle only twelve miles wide seemed overly optimistic indeed. Their lookouts surely would have to be alert and be standing on an upper deck to see such a small speck on their horizon. The Indian Ocean is hundreds of thousands of square miles. And how busy is this shipping lane? Is it even a shipping lane? In any case, ships in wartime take random courses to make it hard for the enemy to find them so we all agreed it was unlikely that we would be spotted. Still, was it the right decision?

Since the rest of the ship's crew and the Captain were in the two boats up-wind to the west and had made no move to get to us and the 2nd Mate was the only deck officer with us, he was in command. "Hundred and fifty miles," he had hollered from the other boat when asked how far to Australia?. The 2nd Mate is the navigation officer on merchant ships and is responsible for plotting the ships course and position.

The situation was discussed. Our distance from Australia and the plight of those on the rafts made it imperative that we go for help. We could not sail upwind to them to take any aboard our boat. What was the Captain thinking?

We were on our own.

With the sails raised and the compass placed securely on the stern seat next to the tiller we pivoted the boats to due east, our wake of swirling water running out straight back to the west. Fast and close hauled, there would be no turning back. Within minutes nothing else was on the horizon, only the other boat struggling to keep up. ----------

Mule Ship

Alone Now

*A*fter a full days sail our progress was being impeded because of the slower boat number one. Lowering our sail every half hour or so we would wait for the other boat to catch up. Why this was so was a mystery. They had 22 men while we had fifteen but also the dead weight of the engine and drag of the prop which should have made us the slower boat.

  Night came and it was even more difficult to keep the two boats together. Losing them in the darkness we would heave-to and flick on a light and wait till they closed the distance. The next morning we started to consider leaving them behind. A day's difference in contacting help could be crucial to those on the rafts. Should we go on ahead and not wait? An agonizing decision. We had extra supplies good for ten days and water. And two boats apart doubled the chance of being in the path of a passing ship or plane on patrol. It again seemed like the wise thing to do.

  About noon we didn't wait. Wondering if we had made a wise decision we watched life boat number one disappear over the horizon behind us.

  That night I discovered that Martinelli couldn't tell left from right! When this quiet little guy, whose mother, no doubt, had told him to never sleep in his clothes and was the only one in thin flannel pajamas, took his turn at the tiller steering the boat, we would find the wind luffing the sail or the boom suddenly swinging wildly. At first, thinking the wind direction had changed suddenly someone would take over and re-set the course. Watching him awhile I could see that he had no idea about which way to push the tiller. The

Dick Sproul

idea of moving it to the right to make the boat turn left was beyond him. And checking the compass heading and putting this all together, well---- he became the designated look-out and no longer had a turn at the tiller. It was no big thing, there were still fourteen,---no thirteen, if we didn't ask the chief engineer to take a turn.

Mule Ship

Thoughts of Home

S*trange*, going through my head over and over again was the tune "Into Each life Some Rain Must Fall" all yesterday, last night and still today. Why is that? Maybe there was a connection but still it seems kind of weird. Aggravating.

During a lull in my re-running of our attack and at the same time that now maddening tune, I thought about when I heard that song. Maybe it wasn't so weird at that.

"Into Each life Some Rain Must Fall". it wouldn't let up!

It was the Mills Brothers at the Florintine Gardens in Hollywood over two years ago and the song was one of many they performed that night. It was a huge place and judging from the crowd there were a couple of other high school proms being held there that night. All those girls, with their colorful prom dresses, pretty nice!

The Mills brothers were almost as popular as the Ink Spots, another Black singing group. They both had hit records out. They had even performed in a couple of movies. I was with Mickie Judd as her date for her senior prom. That too worked out strange, when I thought about it. Two months earlier my cousin Jack had graduated from basic flight training at the El Toro U. S. Army Flight School and planned his wedding immediately afterwards. Jack asked Gene and me to be ushers at his wedding. Gene was now 17 and I was 15. His bride-to-be was Jeannette Haymond who just happened to have a younger sister about my brothers age. Maxine, dark haired, also quite pretty, so naturally a girl Gene quickly latched onto. Or maybe it was the other way

Dick Sproul

around, she latched onto him. That was an ongoing romance.

Maxine however, was a bit of a flirt. Actually, quite a bit of a flirt I was to learn. One evening after dinner at our house I found myself alone on the front porch with her. The porch light was out and it was getting dark. After a few questions from Maxine that seemed, well, a bit forward, she moved closer. More small talk and then even closer. I think she wants me to kiss her! I hesitated but the eagerness of a fifteen year old overcame good sense and I yielded. (Saying I yielded is a cop-out. I was eager!) She responded, enthusiastically! I responded! Then a noise of someone coming. We parted. With a slight look of victory on her face we resumed our casual positions. I don't think I spoke the rest of the evening. If I did I sure have no memory of it.

The wedding was a grand affair. Jack looking spiffy in his 2nd lieutenants uniform and Jeanette in her flowing white wedding dress. Gene and I had new dark, double-breasted suits just bought for the occasion. The church was nearly full.

After the ceremony we all filed out to greet the bride and groom as they headed for the reception. Six of Jack's Air Corps buddies in their crisp Lieutenants uniforms were on the steps in the floodlights, making an arch with ceremony swords. Jack and Jeanette came out of the churcht, ducked under the arch, and were greeted with tossed rice and clapping and cheers.

The punch and cake reception was filled with noisy relatives and friends, some in uniform. Uncle Ed and Dad were holding forth with lively conversation as usual. I had barely finished my piece of cake when Gene and Maxine came over with her cousin Mickie in tow. We're going for a ride why don't you come along? Both Maxine and Mickey were in the wedding party and looked very lovely in their long dresses, eyes sparkling with excitement.

Mule Ship

Gene and I had driven to the wedding in his 32 Ford three-window coupe he had bought a few weeks earlier. The previous owner had already refitted the car with smaller 16 inch wire wheels and that made it look pretty sharp. But the seat would only hold three people and even that would be crowded. There was the rumble seat.

We eased out though the open double doors and I looked back guiltily to see if anyone noticed our departure. I thought I saw mom glance our way but she continued chatting with someone. I took that as permission, sort of. I hoped no one would notice our absence. Uncle Ed would not pass up an opportunity make a public observation of our absence. I always took secret pleasure in his kidding with people but tried to stay out of the line of fire myself and sure did not want to be a target now.

Gene unlocked the car and opened the door for Maxine. "You two get to ride in the rumble seat" she said, with raised eyebrows and an expectant look. I climbed up using the fender step and turned giving Mickey a hand up. I noticed she settled in a little closer than she needed to even in this small seat.

"This is fun, I haven't been in a rumble seat before," she said.

At a loss for words as usual I wondered how this would go and finally managed to blurt out something, probably stupid. Through the rear window I saw Maxine snuggled up to Gene. After only a few blocks Gene slowed and abruptly turned into a side street. He pulled up under a huge overhanging tree that blocked out the streetlight. The engine off, the two heads all but disappeared. There is only one thing to do. I put my arm around this pretty girl next to me. I was smart enough to do that but what do I do next. I knew what I wanted to do but shouldn't I say something first! Mickey broke the ice with "What are the girls like at your school?" I mumbled something and she responded---I have

Dick Sproul

no memory of what we said after that. Only silence from the front seat. An awkward moment passed. Now is the time, move! I told myself and kissed her. She kissed me back! I again did my best imitation of movie stars I had seen, arms carefully around her I tried to be---what? Tender? Yes that was good! Be tender! It seemed to work

But then something new happened. Her lips parted a bit and the tip of her tongue brushed across my lips. Whoa! What was this? Now I had heard kids talking about tongue kissing--French kissing, Yuck!

But this--this was beautiful! A shiver down my spine. It took only a moment for me to respond. More---and better. I fell a little bit in love that night.

Mule Ship

February 11th

*F*ive days now. The weather was perfect for sailing. Wind at our back, moving swiftly up and down huge ocean swells, slicing through white caps and spray in our face. We should see Australia any time now. At the top of each swell all eyes expected to see that thin line of land ahead of us. Each time disappointed. At this speed we must have traveled well over two hundred miles. Taking my turn at the tiller and trimming the mainsail I could hold the boat right at that point where the wake behind us was almost a froth.

Just like Gene and I did when we would sneak that rental boat out of the harbor at Newport Beach.

We'll be there soon! And when relieved of my turn by the next man there was conversation and dreaming.--and maybe a little praying---maybe a lot. My stomach had settled and instead of nibbling and forcing down the rations I looked forward to opening the food locker and the doling out the days meager ration. The first few days I traded food for an extra share of water. I was beginning to wish I hadn't done that. Well, it won't be long now Australia can't be far now. Strange, no birds, no planes. Nothing.

When everyone seemed talked-out, mostly about food now, my thoughts drifted------again.

Dick Sproul

Georgie

"Georgie", George Rosnswieg, lives on the next street across from Sherman's Market on the corner of Hooper Avenue and 77th Place. In the same grade as me and about the same size until the sixth grade when I started to grow taller. Not that that made much difference. I was still a bit afraid of him. Georgie was quick and had a short fuse although he seemed to mellow as he got older and at Edison Jr, High School we became even better friends.

    The thing about Georgie was that it seemed he could do almost anything. And he did do most anything he wanted. His older brother had taught him. The youngest of five with two sisters. Even at age 7 or 8 he knew how to build a campfire, how to tie knots and carve stuff with his pocket knife. When we managed to shoot a sparrow with a BB gun it was Georgie who suggested that we build a campfire and roast it. Of course he knew how to remove the feathers (we boiled water in a coffee can and dunked the bird into it) and how to clean it. He deftly cut off the head and slit it down the belly and cleaned out the entrails. Holding it over the fire impaled on a sharp stick Georgie decided when it was well cooked. With some salt and pepper (quickly obtained from our house) the tiny drumstick that I got wasn't bad. Mostly bone, I picked the small sliver of meat away with my teeth. My mother was horrified when she learned about our "bar-b-que". Of course we would not have mentioned it to her but she insisted on asking what we were doing out there in the vacant lot with her salt and pepper shakers.

    Georgie's constant uniform was ragged overhauls. Often with worn out knees and a torn pocket and one *shoulder strap dangling with a broken buckle. Georgie was, simply, an imp. A prototype. Whatever qualities you want to imbue in an imp, Georgie had. He was quick, very quick, with a temper to match. But most of all he had ideas. The kind of ideas that kept most of his cohorts in awe. He knew how to build a bird trap or a sling shot. How to build a snare from a wild oat stalk that could be used to catch a lizard. How to hypnotize a chicken by placing it's beak on a line in the dirt and stroking its head. (It really works) If Mark Twain had been there he would have instantly recognized Georgie as a latter day Huck.*

Building a campfire was a work of art for Georgie. He would start with crumpled newspaper placed into a shallow depression scooped out of the dirt. Next, kindling was carefully positioned in the shape of a teepee and then larger pieces of wood scrounged from the neighborhood alleys around that. Only one match, carefully shielded from any breeze, was ever needed. A sharpened stick held the marshmallow or hot dog. A potato skillfully packed with mud per Georgie's instructions would bake perfectly in the glowing coals. I was tasked to swipe some butter from my mother's kitchen.

But Georgie's real claim to fame was his running feud with Old Man Cunningham, a big ---all adults were "big"--- beefy Irishman with a shock of gray hair combed over one eyebrow and the beginnings of a sizable beer belly. It seemed he always wore baggy dark pants held up with suspenders over a rumpled tattletale-gray white shirt, often accented with a gravy spotted black vest.

"Gunnyham" as Georgie always called him, owned "The Courts." A strip of small one-room apartments, fairly common in Southern California, that faced an identical set that stretched from our street to the next. Probably built 20 years earlier and badly in need of paint, these flat-roofed clapboard units were Cunningham's domain.

Dick Sproul

Naturally the walkway (actually just dirt) up the middle made a dandy shortcut to the next street. And, naturally, Georgie considered this his shortcut. Just as naturally Cunningham considered this an intrusion and a nuisance to his tenants. The fact that what tenants there were were hardly ever around did not matter.

Of course most of us gave Cunningham and his Courts a wide berth. Georgie did not. Cunningham would come bursting out of his screen door yelling "If I ever catch you, you little S. O. B. you'll be sorry!"---. Well, it happened.

Johnnie Cardoso, my playmate since I was four, the Martin brothers, Howard and Dickie and a kid named Paulie, large for his age, and kinda fat, and I were playing tag on our front lawn. Exhausted and catching our breath, backs flat on the cool green grass under the small struggling Ash tree dad had planted a couple years earlier, content doing nothing but watching white fluffy clouds drift overhead. Then Georgie came briskly up the sidewalk, obviously agitated.

Cunningham had caught him. Marveling at this seeming impossibility we wanted details. It seemed that Cunningham, anticipating Georgie's return trip, had hidden behind the only bush in the otherwise barren passageway. Snagging Georgie, Cunningham had given him a good shaking. With appropriate language I'm sure. That we did not hear this commotion was no doubt due to the racket we had been making.

"I'm gonna get Gunnyham this time. I'm gonna get him good" Georgie hissed. He already had a plan. But he needed our help.

On this otherwise dull day any such plan sounded good to us. He needed a coffee can. A quick search of nearby trash cans soon turned one up.

Georgie had noted that the closing springs on Cunningham's screen door had long since given up and that

Mule Ship

the door was always ajar. A can of water placed on top of the door, a quick knock would do it. What we were yet to learn was that Georgie had a more sinister part to his plan.

We scurried across the street to the house next to the courts where large bushes hid an outside faucet. But after reaching the cover of the bushes instead of filling the can with water Georgie unbuttoned his fly. By now completely caught up in Georgie's clever scheme no one said a thing. In fact some one else also contributed to the can's contents.

The street was empty. With the now half full can, we snuck around the end of the structure. Flattening ourselves against the wall we ducked under the only window. Cunningham's front door was closed and the screen door ajar. Perfect!

But now we had to hoist Georgie up so the he could reach the top of the door. Considering what was in the can, doubts began to creep into our little minds.

"Wait!" Someone whispered. "What if you spill it?"

"I won't spill it" Georgie insisted. "Come on give me a boost" he whispered back.

Reluctantly we grabbed his legs and lifted him. Stretching up, the top of the door was just out of his reach.

"Higher" he hissed. --- We struggled. "Be careful with that can" More whispering. "Shut up, he'll hear us!".

"Clump, clump, clump". Heavy footsteps from inside! Coming towards the door!

We all moved at once like a flock of frightened starlings, leaving Georgie airborne. The can, or rather it's contents, getting us all.

Georgie, being Georgie, hit the ground running. Straight across the street up the Parquet's driveway, afraid to even look back. Through the Parquet's back yard, making for the alley behind the weathered six foot high wooden fence. Surely, Cunningham was right on our tail!

The double gate was closed! Georgie, by now in the lead, scrambled over the weathered and rickety board fence,

Dick Sproul

Johnnie and the Martin boys right behind him. In total panic, I was next to last, Paulie bringing up the rear. Now right on the top I'm about to jump down into the safety of the alley when Paulie hit the fence.

Weightless, the sky, the ground, rotating about me, a loud explosion. I landed in a ball, clear on the other side of the alley against a garage door.

A huge dust cloud filled the alley. Through the dust I see Georgie and the others, frozen in mid stride, looking back, horror on their faces. The entire fence from the telephone pole and including one half of the gate, was now laying flat. Paulie now spread eagled on the flattened fence.

Now what had we done? We will all be arrested and thrown in jail! Down the alley we went, All of us, as fast as we could go. But the end of the alley was too far. Someone will come out and see us! One by one we peeled off looking for a place to hide. Any place. Trash cans, a corner of a garage. We all found a place.

We waited,---- finally peeking out. The alley was deserted, the dust settled. No one came,---it was the middle of the day. Incredibly, no one had heard. No one was chasing us. Slowly we inched our way back up the alley to the fence. No sign of Cunningham.

This was where Nick and John Parquet lived. Older guys.

"They are going to get us for this." was voiced.

"Wait" Georgie said "Maybe we can fix it".

He studied the situation. "Come on!"

With that we all lifted and heaved on the heavy fence and with a mighty surge of determination somehow managed to get it to an upright position. While the rest of us balanced the fence Georgie found a large rock and frantically pounded on the nails that had pulled out at the end where it had been attached to the telephone pole. The gate hasp was hooked up and a stick wedged into it.

"It's still wobbly and will fall right down again."

Mule Ship

Finding more sticks we pounded several into the ground around each rotted post.

"There, that will hold it" Georgie pronounced. We all scurried back up the alley towards my house.

A few days later we're again playing on our front lawn when Nick Parquet comes down the street.

"Hey, guess what guys?"

Oh oh, what's this?

"That wind we had last night, it blew our whole fence down!".

No one said a word. And I don't think Georgie or any of us, ever used the "shortcut" again.

The thought of that little adventure made me think of other things about old man Cunningham. He lived alone in that ramshackle "court" and because of his grouchy reputation few of the neighbors ever talked with him. He must have been lonely. Like I said, whatever tenants occupied those quarters, few were ever seen. A car or two would appear each evening in the open area at the far end of the courts on the 79th street side providing some proof that indeed there were tenants. Other than that the place could have been empty.

Two or three times a week Cunningham could be seen returning from Central Avenue having visited one of the small bars located at frequent intervals along that thoroughfare. His unsteady gait revealing that he had had one too many. Not too long after our water can caper something else happened.

Just after supper we heard a loud crash. Mom had started the dishes and Gene and I were arguing about who was going to "wipe" tonight. Dad was reading the paper. Startled, we all rushed out to see what had happened.

There, across the street, well illuminated by the street light, was a car embedded in the side of Cunningham's

Dick Sproul

street-side apartment. Both doors of the car were open and a man and a women looking a little dazed, standing next to it. A little wisp of steam, probably from a broken radiator was drifting out of the opening. A large group of neighbors were now joining us in the street. Through the opening in the wall we could see what appeared to be a Murphy bed, frame and all, flat on the floor. The room littered with splinters of the shattered wall.

Cunningham, luckily unhurt, was already out on the sidewalk yelling and pointing his finger.

"What are you, drunk? Look what you did to my house!"

I heard my dad chuckling behind me, "Look who's calling who a drunk" he muttered. The couple from the car, obviously intimidated, backed away a step or two. Like us most of the neighbors were crowded around watching this confrontation with some amusement.

The L.A. County Sheriff's cloth-topped touring car soon arrived and with the show now over the crowd drifted back to their homes. It was about time for "One Mans Family" to start on the radio.

Mule Ship

The Draft

Gene turned eighteen three months before he graduated with the Fremont High School class of Winter, '43. He had registered, as required, for the wartime Draft shortly before his birthday. His notice to report for travel for US Army Basic Training indicated a date barely two weeks after graduating.

Mom, Dad and Gene and I all piled into our '36 Ford and drove down to the shiny new Union Station in LA to see him off. It was a Saturday and the station parking lot was nearly full.

On the platform standing next to the train, teary-eyed mom, hugged Gene again and again. Dad, who had made a similar trip 24 years earlier in 1918 was a little misty-eyed too. He had been sent to Ft. Lewis in Washington State while Gene was being sent to Ft. Riley, Kansas. Still sixteen, and more excited about this event than anything else, I looked around to see dozens of other guys standing with their families too, heading off to a new life. This was a scene we had seen re-created in recent war movies as well as real-life movie newsreels. The only thing missing was background music and reporter Lowell Thomas' famous deep, resonate voice.

Gene seemed to be taking it all in stride but somehow a little embarrassed. Here and there were a few others standing alone, unsmiling, suitcases in hand looking a little reluctant to board the train. I wondered what their stories were. Others already aboard were appearing in the train windows. A bit more sober now I gave my brother a sock on

Dick Sproul

the shoulder. I wondered when I would see him again. The train conductor did his "All Aboard" and the rush began.

Minutes later, the train couplings clunked loudly and the loaded cars moved out, hands and heads sticking out of the windows. I couldn't see Gene.

The ride home was quiet.

Mule Ship

School and a Job

School and part-time work at Pachmayer's Gun shop was my routine for the next few weeks. Pachmayer's was on Grand Avenue between 4th and 5th street in downtown LA. Fifty cents an hour was twice as much as I had ever made before. Pachmayer's didn't make guns, but they were well known as expert gunsmiths. A glass counter took up most of the store-front part of the building. Pistols, rifles and shotguns along with scopes and binoculars filled the case. All of the guns were removed each night and locked up even though the front of the building was secured with a window-high expandable metal fence. They had learned their lesson from earlier break-ins.

Wartime demand for small parts for the California aircraft factories not only made the shop a busy place but provided it with priorities to buy additional machine tools as well as draft deferments for key people. However that didn't mean much to me. I was only sixteen.

The 4th of July came and went and then Gene was home. Completing Basic training he had a two week leave and a whole new language. "I'm beat" and "Oh my aching ass" were frequent, never-before-heard phrases. Making the most impact on me was, "Don't join the Army." He hated it. The marching, the KP, the orders from sergeants and especially the officers. "Most of the time there is no reason for any of it. They just give orders because they can. They treat you like you don't know anything."

I got the feeling he thought they were all dumber than he was. Gene did pretty well in school so he was probably right. The most astounding thing of all, he was going to

Dick Sproul

Military Police school. Gene an MP? How in the world did they pick him for that? If ever there was a non-confrontational guy it was my brother! Being a policeman simply was not on his horizon. A lawyer perhaps, but a policeman, never! But there was another side to this assignment. He was going to be an MP Escort Guard. It seemed they needed MPs to guard German and Italian prisoners of war from East Coast ports to prison camps here in the US ---Yeah, that was another thing we had seen in newsreels. Then he was off again to his new duty.

Soon Gene's letters described long train rides from New York and Boston to camps in Illinois and Texas with coach cars filled with German prisoners. He was surprised that quite a few could speak English. Well, I guess I was too. But even more curious information was his exclamation "They are all little guys!" It seemed few of them were over five-foot, ten and most were closer to five-foot, five. At Fremont High School there were only a few guys that small. Most of the guys we knew were at least five-foot ten or more. My buddy, Mike Rizzi, was six-foot like me. Only Georgie, who had stopped growing at five foot eight was, to us, a little guy. Gene was the same height as me and Dad was a little over five foot ten. Most of the guys we knew were, like us, taller than their dads. That was "normal" in our view, at least in Southern California.

I began to hold a whole different view of the vaunted German "Nazis." Hollywood movies always showed them as big, mean guys. That was another thing, Gene said they were mostly polite and friendly and were simply relieved to be out of the war. One prisoner asked how he could get in touch with relatives living in the USA.

Some of gene's letters came that described the Germans as puzzled and a little concerned that their captors appeared to be taking the trains on longer, zigzag paths to confuse them. They were skeptical that it would take three or more days to reach anyplace in the US. They couldn't imagine that America was so much bigger than Germany.

Months went by and my job at Pachmayer's got more boring doing the repetitive production jobs. I was learning more about being a machinist at school and I felt that I could take on more complicated jobs. I finally went to Frank Pachmayer and inquired about a raise. He was busy on a lathe.

Frank was a "working" boss as well as owner. Three people worked in the office upstairs to contact customers and handle the paper work, but most of the time he preferred to be in the shop. His father had started the shop soon after emigrating from Germany after the first World War and he still did some of the more fancy gunsmith work. Particularly orders from Hollywood people. Both Clark Gable and Robert Taylor were hunters and they sent their shotguns to Pachmayer's for customizing. Often with fancy engraving and custom gunstocks added to already expensive shotguns and rifles. The most common customizing was special chokes fitted to the shotgun barrels to keep the shot from spreading out too quickly. Frank also had invented and patented a shoulder cushioning device for rifle and shotgun stocks.

Up on the mezzanine floor of the building were the office and drafting rooms, and a makeshift firing range, actually a hallway stretching from one side of the building to the other. This connected the offices on one side to a bathroom and store room on the other. At the far end of the hallway two layers of sandbags covered with several layers of plywood protected the adjacent building. After a gunsmith completed reworking and reassembling the weapon shotgun firing patterns and the actions of rifle and pistols were tested against target sheets over the plywood.

"Gonna fire!" would be shouted out and "3, 2, 1," counted down so everyone would not be startled at the blast. Then again to assure the weapons performance. Only then it

would be re-cleaned and wrapped, or placed in it's case for the customer to pick up.

One day the FBI brought in a Tommy Gun for cleaning and rework. This was a first the other guys said. But the action was not unlike an automatic pistol. After carefully disassembling and reworking the weapon it was reassembled and Frank took it up to the mezzanine floor for test firing. Only two rounds were loaded into the drum-shaped rotary magazine. "Gonna fire!" and "3,2,1," was loudly shouted out, as usual. "Bam! Bam" and then "Son-of-bitch!"

Everyone stopped what they were doing. Frank came down the stairs with the Tommy Gun and the magazine in the other, a sheepish look on his face. "This thing has quite a kick! The second round went through the ceiling!"

Several of us rushed up the stairs. Sure enough, there was a small, round hole in the ceiling, blue sky shining through! Not said was, "where did that bullet go?" It's a good thing Frank only loaded two rounds or there would have been a lot more holes in the roof!

The Tommy Gun was returned to the FBI without comment, but further jobs of that nature were declined.

The elder Pachmayer, with a huge gray mustache and heavy German accent, had brought a machine from Germany called a pantograph that would duplicate complex shapes like gunstocks. Some customers wanted special features on their weapons or shorter or longer stocks. This machine, now fitted out with a metal cutting tool bit, turned out to be ideal for forming prototype parts for newly designed aircraft. Wooden patterns sent from the aircraft factories were traced by a "stylus" while the small tool rotating at high speed would mirror the stylus movement. My job was to finish-mill the mounting flange and drill holes in these parts.

Mule Ship

Sometimes castings or forgings were hauled in, hundreds of them! Boring! I wanted more challenging jobs. One-of-kind jobs. Jobs that would use the training I was getting at school.

I decided to make my move. A ten cent raise was quickly agreed on but no discussion about the level of work I would perform other than it would continue to depend on the kind of jobs that came in.

After talking with Frank I returned to my work. Hardly a minute had passed when Jerry, one of the fellows who had been with Pachmayer's before I was hired, slipped over to my machine and in a quiet voice ask me what I was talking to Frank about.

Sixteen years old and very naive, I told him I had received a ten cent raise. Without knowing it I had violated protocol. Frank had hired me and so he was the one I went to for the raise. The word got around fast. Jerry was quick to pass it on. It wasn't long before Bob Malore the newly appointed shop foreman came up to me obviously agitated. Except for assigning jobs Bob had barely spoken to me. It seemed that Bob had been negotiating with Frank to get everyone a ten cent raise and he said I had sabotaged his efforts. All the other employees were in on this and were now upset with him because I got a raise and they had not. He was mad as hell and chewed my ass for several minutes before stalking away. This was a totally new experience for me and it wasn't till later that I even thought to wonder why he had not included me in his scheme.

Dealing with Bob was to take another turn.

Not long after that event two very beautiful young women came in at lunch time. One of them was very pregnant. When I say beautiful I'm thinking movie-star beautiful. Both gorgeous blonds. The word was the pregnant one was Bob's wife, the other one was Frank's wife. Lucky guys I thought and sure wasn't expecting what happened later.

It was month or two later I crossed Bob again. Summer vacation and I was working full time and as much overtime as I wanted. As even more work came into the shop new people were hired. In 1943 more women were being hired and trained in factories everywhere. A couple of young girls were hired at Pachmayer's to work the drill presses. After a few weeks I found one of them working next to me. She was quite pretty and well,---- also well stacked and looked pretty good even in coveralls. I learned her name was Shirley and she had just turned eighteen. I told her I was almost eighteen. Actually I had turned sixteen, six months earlier but now had my driver's license and I was sure dad would let me use the car. That she was older than me wasn't a deterrent. I asked her for a date. I sort of knew that with most men between the ages of eighteen and forty in the service most girls were eager for a date, no matter who.

"What should I wear." Shirley asked. That was a good sign. My fantasies took control.

"Something low cut." I couldn't believe I said that. She wasn't fazed.

The Saturday night date went well and ended with a bit more than just a kiss goodnight in the front seat. Still, just high school stuff that I was beginning to learn some girls liked.

Monday and another summer-time sixty hour work week began. Bob comes up to me, fire in his eyes. "I understand you took out my girl!" He glared at me.

"What?" His girl, how can that be?

It took a minute for me digest this. Bob had to be thirty years old or more. What did he mean "My girl"? "You leave her alone, she's mine! I've been dating her. You understand?" Totally confused, no words came to me. What just happened?

Mule Ship

When I got a chance I asked Shirley what she had said to our foreman, Bob.

"He asked where I was Saturday night. He thinks he owns me" she said tartly. A week later she left for another job. I was learning.

Dick Sproul

Where is Australia?

*E*ach day seems to last longer than the day before. Each minute seems to take an hour. We set for two days with no breeze at all, the sea incredibly calm. Four foot swells spread out so we hardly feel the rise and fall. Two small fish, one a ten-inch long baby shark, appeared under our boat seeming to enjoy the shade. We tried whacking at them with an oar or stabbing at them with a splinter of wood carved off of the bench but they just skittered away only to re-enter the shade.

Something we should have done before committing ourselves, we opened up the sealed tube with ocean charts. Each lifeboat is so equipped but since the Second Mate had said "A hundred and fifty miles" along with our approximate longitude and latitude, there was no need. Just sail east. We couldn't miss it. Australia was huge. The shock, and a horrible new awareness, set in. The position, longitude, 100 east, and latitude, 35 south, the Mate had given us was actually seven hundred and fifty miles from Australia!, not a hundred and fifty! How could he make such a mistake? I thought I knew. He didn't. With a few yards separation between the boats and brisk wind and waves the "seven" was swept away and we only heard part of the shout. Still, my thought was we had done the right thing. It would just take another week or more. I was sure we had traveled at least three or four hundred miles. We can do it! Those other lifeboats and rafts might never be sighted. Who knows how long it would take for our ships failure to arrive in port to be noticed? And where would they start searching? The men on

Mule Ship

the rafts must be in terrible shape. I try to estimate how far we've gone. Even with the days becalmed we had to have averaged 50 miles each 24 hours. Maybe more. Of course now I understand why we have not sighted Australia. Fifteen days would be---yes! 750 miles. Any day now! Good signs; an albatross soaring high overhead. How far do they travel?

Disturbing signs; the wind for the last few days comes more out of the south than west. I see our wake angling off, not straight back as the first few days. The army Lieutenant scoffs when I mention this.

"The boats pointed east, that's the way we're going. The compass shows east" He says, as though that proved his point. .

"But we don't have a keel," I protest, "and we are being pushed sideways as much as forward." I look around and see uncertainty on other faces. They don't want to weigh in on this. My only solution would be to rig an outboard keel using the flat surface of the six oars as I suggested on our first day when trying to get back aboard the ship. It would offset some of our sideways drift. If the weather gets too rough we simply take it in. I see no risk. They apparently do. This 33 year old 2nd Lieutenant prevails.

Our conversation now centers on food. We had cut our rations in half. Elaborate descriptions of favorite dishes and when and where we experienced them.

"We have to quit talking about food!

"Yeah, let's talk about girls!"

That lasts for a few minutes until somebody says, "Oh man the last time I was at my girl's house her mother made the greatest pot roast, with potatoes and gravy, -----and we were off again talking about food. That was the conversation. It didn't help, or did it?

Dick Sproul

Harry Edelson

Perhaps I should dwell on something else. Something positive. This brought me to thinking about Harry Edelson. "Coach Edelson". Amazing guy. My senior year was finally here but I had never tried out for varsity sports. My efforts playing ball in the empty lots convinced me that eye-hand coordination was not going to be in my sports talent. I did have strong legs. If they only had bicycling as a school sport I knew I would be a three year letterman, however here I was almost seventeen and having to shave at least twice a week but could only envy the lettermen around school. They looked so great in their cardinal and gray tightly knitted wool coat sweaters, with the letter "F" on the left side and stripes woven into the right sleeve. One for each year playing in three or more games. A three year letterman commanded respect and admiring looks from the prettiest girls. Some guys lettered in more than one sport. Football, track and baseball were the most common. Gymnastics, wrestling and a few tennis emblems identified the other sports available for boys at Fremont High School in the 1940's.

    This was it. My last chance to get a 'letter'. I was going to give it everything I had. At the appointed hour, 3:00 PM, after 6th period I went into the locker room with all the other guys and suited up. I had already signed up and got my physical indicating that I was alive. Sized up by Harry Coffman, the assistant coach, "Soapy" as he as was referred to by some of the team veterans. I never learned how he came by that name. I was handed pads, pants a helmet and a white practice-jersey with "Property of Fremont HS" *stenciled on it. With my brand new 'cleats' in hand, I found a space on a bench. My dad and I had gone out and purchased those size 12 football shoes just the day before. Putting on that uniform I was transformed. I felt invincible.*

'Coach' at about five foot nine was shorter than almost every kid on the team. From New York, he still had a trace of accent even after spending younger years playing football at USC. Along with a trace of Jewish accent, his words had authority and commanded the respect of every player. Of course he was also hard as nails physically and more than once I saw him demonstrate blocking by taking on a six foot tall tackle or guard and knocking him on his ass. This was done without pads or helmet on his part. It was really a bit comical seeing a fully suited player decked out in shoulder pads and helmet, flipped over onto the grass with a surprised look and new respect showing on his face. "You must have determination, with determination you can do it!" I don't think I ever heard him use the word but that he used it twice. With emphasis.

Like I said, Respect.

We all trotted out onto the field where we were put through some warm-up exercises and demonstrations of blocking.

"Keep those legs pumping!" Coach admonished. "That's the way to keep from getting hurt". He was the coach, he knew what he was doing. No one challenged that. Finally, after some of the other linemen were tested, Coach made eye contact.

"OK Sproul, that's you, right?"

I respond quickly. "Yeah Coach", surprised that he knows my name

"Lets see what you can do".

Jack Spencer, a bit shorter than me but 30 pounds heaver was an All-City guard. Already down in his three point stance having just taken on a couple of other try-outs he was ready to test my charge but not expecting much from

Dick Sproul

this "new" guy. Legs spread, right hand on the grass, knuckles down. His left arm bent with elbow forward and a slight grin on his face. Sure, I was intimidated. What was I doing here? The coach's words, uttered a few minutes earlier "With determination, with enough determination you can do it!" still ringing in my ears I took my stance, imitating Spencer's.

How could I expect to look good against this guy? He had just made the two previous candidates look bad.

"Ready?" the coach blew a quick blast on his whistle. I charge, Spencer charges. The banging of shoulder pads and helmets. Spencer has his elbow right in my face. I pump my legs as instructed. I try ignore the elbow and keep pumping those bicycle legs.

I'm holding him! But that elbow is also pumping, right against my nose.

After what seems an eternity I hear the whistle. We both stand up. I taste blood. My blood. Oh no, my nose is bleeding!

I'd had nose bleeds before, no big thing, but I'm crestfallen. I'll be sent to the showers without really showing what I can do! Feeling defeated I'm just about to turn away.

"Let's see that again" Coach says.

I don't dare hesitate and quickly resume my stance, blood now running from my nose. He's giving me another chance!

Spencer now wide eyed, takes his stance again. Again the whistle. We charge. Again the bang of leather against leather. Again the elbow crushing my nose. Blood all over us both. Determination welling up in me I pump those legs. Spencer gives up a step. I'm beating him!

The whistle blows, we separate. The other players are standing there now wide eyed too, wondering how this is going to play out.

"You better get to the showers" Coach says. But I detect a twinkle in his eye,---I've made the team! I now *realize that Coach had used this opportunity to advance all of the team, as well as me, one step closer to manhood. I turned 17 that November.*

We finished that 1943 season beating every team we faced---and I earned my letterman's sweater!

When it was my turn to take the tiller I again had to refocus on checking our course, making sure the compass stayed on the big E and the sail was taking the wind fully. The boat would again heel over and our speed resume. Most of the other guys now had confidence to do the same. Larson and Kent had sailed lifeboats as part of their training on Catalina Island, but even though I missed that class, I relied on my earlier experience. The compass was the only new thing I had to integrate into the process. At the same time unable to stop studying the horizon for some sign, indicating our rescue, or the coastline of Australia.

Another thought of Mickie. Other thoughts of friends, family and adventures, sure, but she had a special place.

I learned at that Senior Prom that she was engaged! Even though she was more than two years older and out of my league, her rush to grow up dismayed me but I was to see this over and over again. She danced very close and I wondered what her friends would think. She didn't seem to care. When I took her home she gave me a long passionate kiss. My night was complete! Perhaps I was, momentarily, some sort of proxy. Not that I minded!

Her fiancé—her long time high school boyfriend—would have a ten day leave after completing his Army Air Corps training as a B17 tail gunner and they were to be married. All this was to take place a week after her graduation.

I didn't expect to be invited to the wedding and I never saw her again, but her story, actually not an

Dick Sproul

uncommon story in these times, swiftly traveled through the family.

After a four day honeymoon her husband left for England.

He was killed on his first mission over Germany. Mickie gave birth to a baby boy nine months after the wedding.

I am planning to be back to tell my own story—I hope.

Mule Ship

Army Air Corps

*T*he Draft still in my future and my interest in model air planes almost entirely blotted out by thoughts of cars and girls and football, not necessarily in that order, the announcement in the LA Times that "men" seventeen and a half-years old could now sign up for U. S. Army Air Corps. 'For pilot training', caught my eye.

Yes! Since my first model airplane I dreamed of zooming through the sky doing loops and turns, barrel rolls, perfect landings and when the war started, shooting down enemy planes. Even before that I would sit in sixth grade class drawing little biplanes complete with machine guns and dotted lines that were my rendition of machine gun tracer bullets.

The Jimmy Allen radio show offered flying lessons via slick illustrated hand-outs available at any Richfield gas station. Exciting movies of the First World War showed men like Eddy Rickinbacker, and other new hero's in this war, shooting down German and jap planes. By now of course I knew that they could shoot back. But I would be always looking over my shoulder, ever alert. They would never catch me!

And from those hand-outs I knew about G-forces, control stick and rudder movements as well as almost every thing else about aviation. I pored over magazines like Aviation News, Popular Science and Model Airplane News. They had articles about the newest aircraft and engines in development. Even pieces about weather and navigation. I learned about control surfaces and their reaction to flowing air. I even built a model of a 1930s Boeing P 26-A fighter aircraft with a control stick and threads running out to the wings and tail. I could stick my finger into the cockpit and move the small control stick connected to the ailerons and tail surfaces and imagine the aircraft responding to my control. Move the stick to the right and the right aileron would go up and the left go down for a bank to the right for a perfect turn. Back and the elevator surface would come up and I could see, and almost feel the loop with me strapped into the cockpit.

Early in the morning on the day announced in the paper I drove into LA and parked near the building where the sign-up was to occur. Soon there were over fifty guys waiting for the doors to open.

We filed into a large class room and given papers to fill out. They announced there would be two 2 hour tests before a break for lunch and then a physical.

"All right, open your test books" was ordered. Wow! There were over a hundred questions. With great concern I dug in. But wait, this was stuff I already knew. Questions about air resistance, wing loading, lift and thrust and drag. Questions about cumulus, cirrus and stratus clouds, up-drafts and down-drafts. Some of the questions I had doubts about. Carefully going back over the answers I checked everything. Time was running out! Some had closed their books and left the room. Boy! Those guys must be smart.

"Time!" I had used every minute and wished I had more. I reluctantly turned in my first answer sheet. A twenty minute break and we started again.

This time there were different sections devoted to how you felt about things and diagrams to figure out. Some were circuit diagrams, others were connect-the-dots type of problems only much more complicated than any I had seen before. Some Algebra this time. A couple of the word problems I couldn't get. Again I carefully re-checked

Mule Ship

everything and again I wished I had more time. I looked up and the room was almost empty.

We were excused for lunch. With a couple of other guys I walked over to the Pig and Whistle restaurant on Broadway.

Back in the room it went this way;

"We thank you all for coming in today. We have graded the tests and most of you did pretty well." That was a good sign.

"If I don't read your name you didn't pass. If I do read your name please go to room 303 down the hall after a break for lunch and take your physical. Be back by one o'clock. There was one score, ninety four, almost ten points higher than any other," he announced. I wonder if we will know who that was?

"Which one of you is Sproul?" Stunned, I tentatively held up my hand. Did this mean what?

"You had the best score." He said with raised eyebrows. I floated out of the room. I had passed! I had passed! With the best score! Amazing. The best grade I had ever received in school was a B-plus in shop class.

But it wasn't over yet. I tested 20/30 vision, not quite good enough. They wanted only 20/20. Crestfallen, to put it mildly, I drove home to tell mom and dad.

And here I am, in this lifeboat.---------- We cut the daily ration to half a can of pemmican and one cup of water.

After graduation I worked again full time at Pachmayers and bought a 39 Ford convertible, customized with a nosed- off hood and twin pipes. I had until November till I turned eighteen and be drafted, probably into the army. Most of the guys with me all through school had already turned eighteen and were quickly gone. Mike Rizzi, Jim Williamson, and a couple of others, like me, had the whole summer before we had to go. George Rosenswieg,

Dick Sproul

"Georgie" I was surprise to learn was older and left the week after graduation, only to show up four weeks later, in his army uniform, from Basic Training. My brother had to complete Basic before he got any leave.

"They said that anyone who was Jewish could get leave for the Jewish holiday" he explained. Of course Georgie was as far from being Jewish as any of us. Leave it to Georgie to work the angles.

Mike continued, like me, to work at the new job he had; but for me football beckoned.

Come September, Jim and I enrolled at Compton Jr. College. Three courses was all I needed to be eligible to play. We knew we wouldn't finish the semester, but who cares, we might make it through the football season! Dad didn't know what to think about this scheme. Especially since he had loaned me half of the money to buy the car. Of course I had to quit my job to attend school and for football practice.

I did get a part-time job at Sears mounting tires and installing batteries. Tires were rationed but quite few people were getting approval. Jeep tires of synthetic rubber were becoming surplus and so were the most often mounted.

At Compton, well, this wasn't High School! First thing I noticed was the short skirts the cheer leaders wore. At Fremont High School we didn't have cheer leaders, only the girls drill team, with skirts below the knee. To be fair, they did win awards for their precision marching.

There was the Student Union where you could hang out. Neat! And at registration wearing my letterman's sweater Coach Tay Brown intercepted me on the steps to the administration building.

"You going out for football? He eagerly asked.
"Sure."
"What position."

Mule Ship

"I played right guard." I thought his smile weakened a bit.

"OK tell the people at the desk. They'll sign you up and give you a practice schedule."

Wow, was this great or what!

Reality set in. In the locker room at the first practice there were guys, big guys, older guys. This sure wasn't High School. Some of them were veterans. The war now ending its third year and campaigns in both the Pacific and in Europe turning in our favor, some of these guys had been discharged from the service on a 'point' system. Three or more years, seeing combat and other factors made it possible to request discharge.

One other thing; a few of these guys were black. A very new thing for me. Black people were out there of course, but somehow I had never known a Negro. Only stories, usually not good. There was Kenny Washington a black football star that played for USC, and Black people who had become famous for different reasons but to me they were another world. I think I was a little afraid of them. What would I say to a black person?

But work-outs and practices were what they were. Suited-up it didn't seem to make any difference. I soon found myself relegated to the Jr. Varsity squad. The first string would run plays against us. It was brutal at first but gaining experience and strength it got better, somewhat. And I had signed up and I was going to see it through. Playing San Diego Navy was really tough. I didn't see a single guy under 25. And these were their forth string against our fourth, or "Jr. Varsity."

My last game was against Pasadena Jr. College. Gas rationing turned out to be a problem. Not having gas for the football team to use the school bus, coach Brown announced we would have to car-pool. My convertible's engine was disassembled and spread out on our garage bench so I would have to get a ride. Sterling had a car. A small, very

Dick Sproul

small, Willys 77, about a 1935 model. That was OK, he had used little of his gas ration and invited me to go along. Fine! Sterling was a "bookish,"-- that was my mother's favorite term -- kind of guy and my thought was he didn't seem like the type that would go out for football.

We started to pull away with the other cars when Sterling spotted a lone teammate who didn't seem to have a ride. A slim, tall black guy. Of course I had seen him at practices and games, but never talked to him.

"Hey! You need a ride? Sterling shouted out. "We've got room for one more." I should have expected it. That's the way he was. He was a bit like my brother, always asking questions and getting opinions. The fellow gave what I thought was a relieved smile and came toward us. I was immediately apprehensive. I had never sat close to a black person before and we would be jammed into this dinky automobile! I quickly jumped out and held the door open. I sure didn't want to be squeezed in the middle. Fortunately we were all narrow enough to fit. Closing the door against my thigh and we were on our way.

"You're Andrew, right?" Sterling quickly asked. I too had heard his name called out by the coach but there were 40 or more guys out there on the practice field and I hadn't made that much of an effort to remember many of them. This led to the next question, "Where you from"?

At least a year or older than I, and an inch or two taller, Andrew paused a minute and then said "Illinois, near Chicago."

The next obvious question, "What brings you out here?" and other gentle prodding brought out Andrew's story. He had joined other black men wanting to serve by joining the Army Air Corps as part of the Tuskegee Institute's Pilot's training program for black men.

Six weeks into the program he got his first weekend pass. Eager to see the town, he put on his dress uniform and headed out on the two mile walk to the small city. About

Mule Ship

halfway there he encountered other black trainees rushing back to the base. It seems one the military wives living in town had been thrown off a bus by the white driver and had broken her arm. Hearing of this her husband went into town, found the driver and beat him up. Crowds of white men were searching for the soldier. The frightened soldiers were getting to safety.

Andrew, deciding he wasn't part of this and really looking forward to this pass, continued to town. Approaching the town square he saw a large crowd with a black soldier in their midst. He was bound and they were yelling and beating him. Now frightened too, Andrew sought refuge in the bushes. A terrifying sight followed. The enraged crowd lashed the man to a tree and took a blow torch to his crotch and burned the bloody and dying man.

Now I had read about lynchings and other terrible things that happened in the South and that was a different world to me, but here I was hearing it first hand. I also knew that it was wartime and some things were hushed up, with even the newspapers not wanting to make a big thing of an event that would hurt morale.

I believed him. He said he and others having direct knowledge of what happened were given a quick discharge and sent home. His commanding officer recommended he not go home where a lot of questions might be asked and suggested he come to California, where he had relatives, which explained his presence here.

The rest of the trip seemed quick but we were the last ones to arrive. We hurriedly piled out and into the locker room of the Pasadena Rose Bowl. This was the field where their Jr Varsity played some of their games. The thrill of actually playing in this famous spot somewhat muted by the new real world we had just stumbled on. I remember we had to finish the game before dark. The glow of the stadium lights would make a dandy back drop for Jap submarines lurking off the coast. We won that game, 20 to ten. There

Dick Sproul

were about 35 people in the stands. I don't think there were any from Compton.

Mule Ship

The Burglar

I came wide awake when I heard mom gasp. "There's someone in our house! See, the curtain is pulled back. I straightened it just before we left!" One of my earliest memories. We had just stepped out onto the porch of our neighbor's house across the street. Invited over for a bridge game, my folks had decided it was time to leave. Gene and I had started to fall asleep so mom was struggling to guide us out the door and home to bed. Mr. Lillybridge, young, robust but on crutches from an accident he had on his job as a truck driver, turned to his wife. "Call the police! I mean the Sheriff!". They were probably one of the few people on the street with a telephone and we lived just outside the Los Angeles City limits so it would be the Sheriff who would respond.

Dad said "I'll go around to the back and check"

"I'll check the front door" said Lillybridge. Across the street they went, Lillybridge bumping rapidly across the pavement and up the front steps, while my mother herded my brother Gene and I back inside. Peeking out the window we watched Dad disappear into the dark space between our house and the house next door.

Now at our door I could see Mr. Lillybridge trying the door handle.

Minutes went by.

Then everything seemed to happen at once. Red light shining, a sheriff's car pulled up just as Dad appeared coming down our driveway dragging something behind him. Porch lights came on and neighbors poured into the street surrounding dad and the sheriff's car. Mom, Mrs. Lillybridge, Gene and I trailing behind, rushed out.

Pushed to the back of the crowd I strained to see something.

"Please step back folks!" One of the officers commanded. The crowd barely moved.

I caught a glimpse of dad holding a petrified black guy, actually just a kid, a spot on the back of his head wet with blood. More people were gathering, pushing, crowding for a better look.

Wasting no time the officers hustled the handcuffed kid, went through his pockets but found nothing except a pocket knife. The officers shoved the kid into the back of the patrol car, flipped on the siren and sped off.

I heard my dad exclaim, "Damn, if I knew he had that knife I might have grabbed him differently."

Completely bewildered by this string of events the next thing I remember was being tucked into bed.

Listening to dad talking with the neighbors the next day I pieced together the details of the night's events. As he peeked around the back of the house he saw the cut window screen lying on the ground. Just then the intruder leaned out, looking the other way towards the driveway. Taking three quick steps to the window Dad grabbed him, yanked him out of the window, slammed him to the ground and landed on top of him. Dad jumped up and took the fellows legs pulling him towards the driveway.

Next day a Sheriff came to the door and took a statement from Mom. That was it.

Life went on. Except for a comment now and then I never heard any more of it. As I got older I often wondered what happened to the fellow. I would never know.

Waiting, thinking, each night was the longer, each day was even longer, the horizon disappointing me each time

Mule Ship

I looked up. Thirst and hunger no longer a craving, just a general weakness---or something.

Dick Sproul

Often thinking about my cousins and Uncle Ed's farm other adventures came into my thoughts:

A Week on the Farm

More athletic than most guys and in high school now, Jack, the youngest of four, was into gymnastics. It figured. Every morning and evening he and his older brother Duane loaded thirty or forty, five-gallon milk cans onto the truck for transport to the commercial dairy for pasteurizing and bottling. This, along with other farm work, made them both pretty strong. But it was Jack who had unloaded the hay bales from the feed supply truck and stacked them in the barn, six or seven high. Using a couple of bale hooks, each about 18 inches long with a cross bar oak handle, he would heave each bale up onto the first layer of bales then jump and heave it again up another layer. I had watched him do this the year before. At 7 years old I could barely lift one end. But this year Gene and I were going to stay for two whole weeks with our cousins. Dad had been out of work for a couple of weeks and our cupboard was getting bare. He had found a new job but it would be a week before he got his first paycheck. Uncle Ed offered to have us stay at his dairy farm.

Previous visits were usually just for the day or maybe overnight on weekends so we were thrilled to spend an entire two weeks of the summer. Every time we visited there was something to see or explore. Jack's oldest brother, Duane, was studying chemistry and Bert was interested in astronomy and had just completed building a twelve-inch telescope. The craters on the moon and the rings of Saturn were new sights for us. An air compressor and tools in the pump house, along with a gas pump outside, made the farm even more self-

Mule Ship

sufficient and provided my cousins with even more opportunities to experiment.

The next morning the milking started before dawn. Fresh milk right off the chiller is a treat few get to relish. Rich and creamy it's a taste to never forget. As soon as the dairy truck was loaded Jack took us in tow. "Come on guys, I want to show you something." We followed him into the barn.

As barns go, this barn was larger than most. It had a corrugated iron hip-roof with STOCK YARDS painted in large black letters on the side easily seen from the highway. Inside the barn there was this years supply of hay, bails neatly stacked, filling one whole side. The top layer was much higher than my head. Near the open door was a gap in the very bottom layer.

Hollering "follow me" Jack dove into the opening.

"Come on!" he urged from inside the narrow tunnel.

Tentatively, Gene and I looked in. We could see Jack about five feet in, at a corner of the tunnel. In we went. Jack scurried ahead, "it goes up here." In the now very dim light I could barely make out the wall of hay in front of us and the dark opening above. The smell of the bailed hay now growing stronger with each move. Ahead of us Jack's voice continued to urge us on. "We go right and then left here." we could hear him some distance ahead of us. In total darkness we felt our way with growing excitement. This was fun. A couple of more turns and then up another level. What a great tunnel!

"I hope we don't run into any rats." Jack's voice, now seeming to come from behind. He was just fooling wasn't he? But maybe not! And how did he get in back of us? The tunnel must loop back somehow. Gingerly feeling the sides of the hay bales we moved on.

"Wait" Gene said. "It goes three ways here." I squeezed up along side him. I could feel emptiness above and on each side. Which way to go? Now a bit concerned, I hope *we can find our way out of here. Now nothing at all from Jack. Absolutely dark---absolutely quiet. We decided to go to the right.*

"I hope this is the way." We kept going. Another turn. Still nothing from Jack. How long have we been in here?

Finally, Jack's voice. "Are you guys lost?" It came from somewhere ahead of us.

"We're coming." At the next turn we could see some light. We hurried on and popped out at the same end of the barn but above where we had entered.

"Wow, that was neat." Gene said.

"Were you guys scared?"

"Naw" I said.

"Well, I knew you were not going to leave us in there all day." Gene rationalized.

Duane appeared in the doorway. "So here's where you guys are! Come on it's time for breakfast."

Yeah, I was beginning to think that very same thing.

When first told, Duane's story didn't make much of a impact on me, but this family ---legend?---made me wonder. The Sproul family were among the founders of Norwalk, California and Uncles Gilbert and Atwood---dad's great uncles, made the trip from Oregon to Northern California upon learning gold had been discovered. Earlier migration from Maine to Oregon took place just before the opening of railroad connecting the nation. I remember old cardboard mounted photographs of the two in long black dusters and black hats. Dark heavy beards and mustaches completed the image. They had brought their found gold to southern California and purchased a large piece of land that had become Norwalk. Just how my uncle Ed became owner of a portion of that land I had never learned. Maybe someday I'll ask.

Mule Ship

Duane was eight years older and of course had chores as most farm kids did as soon as they were old enough. Plowing with a team of mules was taken on at about nine or ten.

About the time when I was born in Los Angeles he was already an experienced hand and no doubt could plow a straight furrow. The mules were strong and obeyed every command. So---the story goes,--- Duane was plowing a freshly cleared field south of the house turning the soil for planting when he heard a faint clink. With a "whoa" the mules halted with one foreleg suspended, frozen. Duane looked back at upended soil. Something glittered in the bright afternoon sun.

Bailing off the metal plow seat he stooped down and dug a silver dollar out of the dirt. Under that was another! Frantic digging with his hands exposed a weathered-torn burlap sack loaded with more silver dollars. The mules waiting patiently, he stuffed the whole hoard in his shirt, got back on the plow, finished to end of the field and headed back to the house.

Not saying a word to anyone he quietly climbed the stairs to his bedroom and unloaded the sack. Exactly 50 coins, dated from the 1880s and 90s.

Uncle Ed, finally curious about Duane's spending trips to the General Store, got the story out of him.

This day, like the days before, is forever, the horizon still empty. But then the night, even longer. Maybe if I had an interest in astronomy and study the stars? If only I could sleep---------try to think of the good things.

Like when as a ninth grader, I finally got my first kiss. Turning 14 in November and shaving the darkening fuzz on my upper lip for the first time was a milestone but unlike most of my friends, ------- I was afraid of girls. The prettier the girl the more afraid I was, afraid of making a fool of myself----which of course I often did.

I was in no hurry to grow up. But here it was New Years Eve and the Fox Theater was having a midnight show and I wanted to go. On a previous evening at the theater, seated in the row behind, I had enviously watched a classmate, pudgy Lee Pyle, kissing cute dark-haired Ruth Higgenbottem. I yearned to take his place but never got that chance. Who would want to kiss me anyway? Most girls I knew were friendly but did they see me as someone like that? How would I ever know?

But now here I was, watching kids gathered at the front of the theater while a movie clip of New Years Eve festivities played and the seconds counted down. It was 12 midnight. Some girls and boys started kissing. I recognized some of the faces but no one that I knew. As I came near the group I stood there feeling awkward. Suddenly a very cute girl (as I am prone to remember) disengaged herself and looked around. She turned toward me.

"Oh I haven't kissed you!" With that she tilted her head and laid one on me, softly and lingering. A really good one! I tried to imitate embracing her just like I had seen actors do in the movies. What a wonderful feeling! A girl in my arms, it was really happening!

With a "Hey, not bad!" she turned, apparently looking for another target. It was a few moments before I regained my senses. But she was gone, melted into the crowd. I never saw her again. But that was OK, my confidence is now firmly established and fantasies of all the other girls I would now try to kiss surged through my mind. That girl, that anonymous adventurous girl, will never know what she started.

Mule Ship

Letting my mind drift helped, but each day was a lifetime, especially when the breeze fell off to almost nothing. We saw our first bird, high up, wings out, motionless, soaring on the summer air. Headed west. We were headed east. It had a long, split tail and some called it a Man-O-War bird, others said it was an Albatross. Where was it going? Where had it come from? What did it mean? It didn't help when someone said they were seen hundreds of miles at sea. We cut our rations down again. The pemmican cans divided up four ways now, malt tablets four to each man. Water, carefully divvied up in the porcelain covered measuring cup that was part on the lifeboat's gear.

For the first time in my life I had time, lots of time, to think. Rather than living each day as it came, now I was forced to think, to remember. Mostly about the good times.

Dick Sproul

The Invention

I remembered The Big Invention. There was this older kid, Kenny Walmsley, older than Gene I think, he lived on 77th Place, the next street over. One day Kenny comes by carrying a reel of movie film and an old hand crank projector. His dad had brought it home from his job at a film studio in Hollywood. The beat up projector did not have a take-up reel nor did it have a light bulb. Scrounging a bulb from our kitchen cupboard, we eagerly set up the projector in the wash shed in our back yard. The only place where there were no windows but still had an electrical outlet. The spot of light on the white washroom wall was weak but it would do. After several attempts we got the film threaded the right way through the mechanism and with steady cranking are able to view the film. The image is only a close up of some man who appeared to be talking! His mouth is the only thing moving. This is disappointing. We keep cranking but still the same guy, still talking. Soon we have a large pile of film on the floor and no easy way to get it rolled up again. This was no fun! What else can we do?

"Wait," Kenny wailed, "What are we going to do with this mess?"

"What? Does your dad want it back?"

"Naw, he just wanted to show me. He said it was going to be thrown out"

We take pity on Kenny and set about retrieving the film. Since there is no way to crank it backwards we set about tediously turning the reel backwards until all the film is back in place. We talk a while about what we could do next.

Mule Ship

"I wonder how this stuff would burn?" Georgie asks. "I heard movie film burns really fast."

"OK, let's cut off a piece and see." Says Kenny.

I run back into the house and grab a pair of scissors and some matches from the match box next to the stove. On the large bare spot in the middle of the empty lot next door the foot long piece of film flares brightly leaving only a blackened trace in the dirt.

"Wow!" Georgie says, "This stuff burns like gunpowder." Now how Georgie knows this bit of information is unknown but none of us are about to reveal our lack of experience here.

"I bet we could make a skyrocket out of this." Georgie always has the greatest ideas. "You know Fourth of July skyrockets are just gun powder inside a paper tube."

Of course we all know this, don't we?

"What will we use for a tube?"

"Just wrap in it layers of paper." Again Georgie's wisdom.

Cutting off another foot of film we roll it as tightly as we can into a half inch cylinder. Over that we carefully wrap it with layers of newspaper torn into three inch wide strips. Twisting each end secures the assembly.

"We better do this in the middle of the street. Those weeds could catch fire." I'm the worrier here, after all, my house is right next to the empty lot. Quickly moving into the street the "rocket" is set down on the pavement and one end of the twisted paper is lighted. The small flame burns for a second or two.

Startled, we all jump back as the rocket hisses and takes off. Only it doesn't go straight. For a few seconds it whirls in tight circles. Only a slight stink and a little ash remain.

"Hey! Let's try it again."

The next attempt starts the same but this time it whirls toward a parked car. This could be a big problem.

Dick Sproul

Frantic efforts are instantly made to stomp it out. After several attempts someone catches it squarely with their heel. That stops it, but wait, now smoke pours out, clouds of foul smelling smoke! Great clouds of stinky rotten eggs smoke! The first rocket had only burned for a few seconds but this one continued smoldering for a full minute.

This was great! We quickly made up another one and tested it. Now the street was filled with smoke, a light wind moved the cloud along. Quickly moving up-wind we marveled at our creation. We had invented a stink bomb!

I really don't want to think about what we, a bunch of 10 and 12 year olds, did with this invention!

Mule Ship

The Neighborhood

LA *City hall was completed in 1928 and dedicated in April of that year.*

Civic center expansion was in progress and houses built in the 1890s, and some more recently, were moved to make room. Over the years several of those houses were moved onto lots on our street. First was a three bedroom bungalow style placed next to our house and the Dobson family, one nearly grown boy, moved in. Shortly afterwards a Victorian style house was moved to a lot east of our house and the Parquet Family moved in,---about 1931. Nick, the youngest, and Johnny, Bernice and Rosemary. I never saw their dad. Nick was in the same class with my brother Gene, while the other Parquet kids were older, teenagers. Then the house moving stopped until 1935, wthen Mike Rizzi's family had an 1890s house moved to the front of their property after living for years in the small two-bedroom bungalow placed in the rear of the 130 foot deep lot. Other families included more kids, the Neverka's, the Oswald's, the Cardoso's, and others that made up the many changing games, and occasionally some border-line mischief.

That was the neighborhood I knew.

Dick Sproul

Oregon Summer

And I thought about the summer of '41, the big adventure in my life--- *until now I guess. I hope this turns out to be an adventure.*

    Graduating from the Edison Junior High school 9th grade the big plan was to visit cousin Bob in Oregon. Uncle Charlie had died the year before and Aunt Rose, Bob and his new bride Violet had paid us a visit. Bob had taken over the ranch and had turned it into a prosperous venture, and an invitation to visit got my attention. Bob had stories about horses and cattle, and as a guide hunting deer. With a pack mule and horses he took parties of business men from Portland or Eugene back into the hills for a week of camping and hunting.

    "I charged them each ten dollars a day, a pack horse and grub," and added; "I guaranteed each would get a deer--- even if I had to shoot it myself," he added, with a wink.

    Violet told a story about a deer that appeared across the road from their house, just standing there looking at them. Bob immediately got a rifle. Violet, taking pity on what appeared to be friendly animal, told Bob that she wanted to shoot the deer, fully intending to simply scare it off. She casually pointed the rifle in the general direction and pulled the trigger.

    The deer dropped dead. We all laughed at her misadventure.

    Hearing these and other stories I sure wanted to see a real cattle ranch, ride horses and go deer hunting .Things I had only dreamed about.

Mule Ship

Dad allowed that it just might be possible. We now had the 1936 Ford which could make the trip, and with the couple of week's vacation he was going to get, we could do it. But later, after he realized that the car would need new tires, and that two weeks weren't nearly enough, the trip was canceled.

Then an opportunity appeared. Our neighbors were going to drive to Seattle and could drop me off in Eugene. I had money saved from my job at Pratt's restaurant and could buy a bus ticket to Mt. Vernon, a small town in Oregon where Aunt Rose lived and was the Post-Master there. Bob's ranch was a few miles up the road toward Pendleton, Oregon, near a place called Fox Valley. And, I had enough money to buy a train ticket for the trip home.

I caught the late afternoon bus heading east toward my summer adventure. After winding through forests and strange forbidding lava fields it got dark and the driver stopped at a small town for the night. Retrieving my new but cheap suitcase I went into the dimly lit bus station. The few other passengers and the driver scurried off into the night leaving this 14 year old wondering what to do next. Two grizzled men, chairs propped against the wall, were the only occupants.

"Where can I find a good hotel?" I asked.

"Thee hotel is right around the corner," one responded starkly. I felt a little foolish, of course this small town might have only one hotel. Maybe I was lucky that it had one!

Sure enough, a small dimly-lighted sign on the darkened street said just that, Hotel. Two dollars and a promise I would be awakened before the bus left secured the night's sleep.

Thinking of my summer in 1941 at Cousin Bob's ranch and of all things that happened, perhaps my understanding of "animal husbandry," was expanded. But

Dick Sproul

why do they call it that? I only think of the term because my brother took an elective, "Animal Husbandry" in Jr. High School. I think they raised a baby rabbit. So when Bob herded a heifer in from the range that was having difficulty, what unfolded next certainly created an image that I expect will stay with me forever. As soon as the cow entered the corral it collapsed and lay there heaving breath. We all gathered around.

"It's coming out backwards." Bob announced

Sure enough two small hooves and a wet slimy bit of tail protruded from the rear end of the cow. Bob squatted down and grasped the little legs to give the heifer some help. The legs and more of the tail slipped out then stopped. Bob stood up and studied the scene.

"Go in the barn and get the block and tackle. And some rope!" He added.

Quickly he fastened a half hitch around the yet to be born calf's legs and secured the block and tackle to the base of a fence post. Together we gave a pull, but all we managed was to slide the heifer a few inches causing her to bellow loudly. The calf was stuck. Again Bob paused to consider what might be next. The nearest Vet was over 30 miles away in John Day. The only way to get him here was to make the trip, assuming he had not been called away somewhere else. There was a telephone in Mt Vernon but that would take the better part of an hour just to hope the Vet was available.

"I've got to turn it around," he said and hurried over to the house. I wondered just how he supposed he could do that? In a minute or two he returned with a basin full of water followed by Violet holding a bottle of Lysol. Rolling up his sleeve he thoroughly washed his hand and arm clear above his bicep. He next pushed the calf's legs back into the cow followed by his hand and arm almost up to his shoulder. Now he also was laying on the ground almost becoming a part of the cow. The cow's tail began thrashing wildly.

Mule Ship

"Hold that tail!" he shouted. I grabbed it and held fast.

Grunting and straining he finally began to pull his arm, dripping with goo, out from the depths of the cow. In his fist two small hooves again appeared, this time the forelegs, I hoped. The block and tackle was reattached. Soon the head appeared and the now-dead calf slid out.

"Well I didn't think the calf would make it but I sure hope I don't lose the heifer too. We'll just have to wait and see," he finished.

I was due to leave on the "Stage", actually the Mail truck, the only transportation to Pendleton, Oregon where I was to catch the train home to start my freshman year in the tenth grade at Fremont High School.

The heifer staggered to her feet, turned, sniffed the dead calf and stood there looking as sad as a cow can look.

I never did learn if she lived. Why now have I thought of that day?

Summer at Bob's--Working at Fox Valley--Living at their house--Spud and Anita and Linc, Violet's young nephew and niece and brother. Herding horses down the road, it was Highway 395 from Mt. Vernon to Pendleton,---------I was Lead and rode ahead to flag down cars so they would slow for the small herd. Mid-day and we had encountered only a couple of older cars chugging along after a couple of miles of fairly straight road. As we came to a sharp curve I lost sight of Bob and Linc and the horses behind me. A shiny new Buick comes clipping along and I waved. The driver waved back and zoomed around the curve. A screech of brakes and a loud thump--I wheeled my horse around and galloped back. A horse was down and the car, driver and Bob looking anxious. Bob yelled for me to go back and stop any more cars. None appeared. After awhile I heard a distant 'pop' and soon they came around the bend, short one horse. Bob had put the horse out of its misery with *the rifle he always carried in a scabbard on his saddle. I learned later that the driver had stopped in Mt. Vernon and left 35 dollars at the post office as payment. Bob said that was fair.*

And finally, too soon, the return trip—the "Stage" to Pendleton. Train to Salt Lake City. Train to LA via Las Vegas,---a late-night 30 minute stop in that sleepy little town, dark except for a glow in the distance from the new Flamingo Casino where its owner, mobster Bugsie Segal had been shot a few months earlier.

Home the next afternoon, my summer adventure was over.

Too tired, yet sleep doesn't come. Or have I slept without knowing it?

As little kids we loved to ride downtown on the 'S' car to see the Christmas windows that all the big department stores displayed. The most intriguing were those animated. Santa's with waving arms, elves in sleighs sliding down slopes, electric trains, all this was new. We grew older, too old it seemed for this kid stuff. Still, I retained a bit of wonder and longing.

The Sunday Comics at first read to us by dad before I learned to read, but then it seemed I could read them myself. Gasoline Alley, Dick Tracy, Katzenjammer Kids, Mickey Mouse-Donald Duck and Little Orphan Annie, and saving cereal box tops eagerly sent away for a 'Secret Decoder Badge.' I wonder what I did with that badge? Flash Gordon and Buck Rodgers and Little Abner started in the Sunday Comics. With a muscular "Lil" Abner, a voluptuous Daisy Mae and the residents of "Dog Patch" the humor was clever

Mule Ship

and often mirrored current events. There was Senator Claghorn, a blustering politician and "Mammy Yokum" who, when it came down to it, could whip about anybody. Fun with a clever level of satire often worked into the stories. "Blondie, Barney Google, and Bringing Up Father," which changed into "Maggie and Jiggs" at some point. One strip I liked was "Abby and Slats," a young brother and sister who's carefree father was always needing rescue. One time they had to travel to some place called Afghanistan where he was being held captive.

In 1941 a new type of strip started in the LA Times. "Prince Valiant" was carefully drawn, almost like an etching. Life-like drawings of mid-evil knights, castles and horses. Wonderful stories of adventures in Camelot with King Arthur. Other "adventure" strips started about this same time. Terry and the Pirates put a young adventurer in the path of Chinese War Lords.

Strange, where the mind goes------this trivia occupies my mind perhaps? But it doesn't stop the constant search of the horizon, even at night.

Again that thin strip of fire appears where the sharp line drawn by the water and the sky identifies the horizon. Then larger and intensely brighter, we have to look away, that "sun thunder" that Kipling in his powerful prose imaged, to begin yet another segment of our now endless torture. The torture of boredom. Boredom laced with fear. Hunger that had been replaced with lethargy.

Mule Ship

Photos

Dick Sproul

Sproul Home on E. 78th St. in Los Angeles, next to the empty lot

On Catalina Island, December, 1944. Dick Sproul on left.

Mule Ship

Crew Dick trained with at the US Maritime School on Catalina Island. The little cabins were salvaged from the 1932 Los Angeles Olympics to create 'The Village.' He lived on, 'Easy' Street (Easy for the military phonetic alphabet 'E').

Catalina Island, Avalon Bay, December, 1944

Dick Sproul

SS Peter Silvester before she was outfitted to carry Army mules

A Sister Liberty Ship, built in one week by welding prefabricated parts together.

Mule Ship

Pre-fab section of a Liberty ship on a trailer on its' way to the San Pedro shipyards, while passing Dick's high school in 1943.

This booklet was distributed to Merchant seamen during WW II. This was my second copy after the first was lost when the SS Peter Silvester was sunk in the Indian Ocean in Feb., 1945. The ship was named after a NY Representative who served in the 1780's.

Dick Sproul

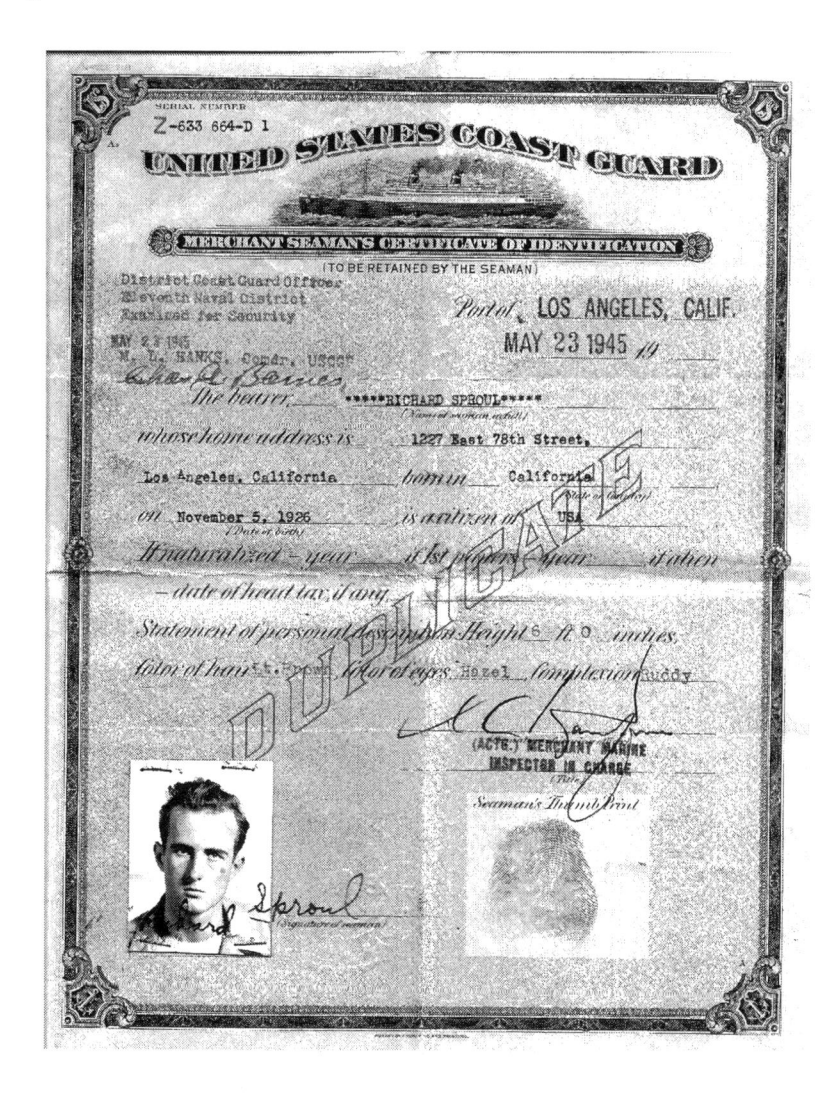

s

Mule Ship

Crew of Lifeboat #2 or #4 rescued after three days

Crowded conditions on Lifeboat #1

*Lifeboat #1, where Sproul was assigned
(But ended up on Boat #3)*

Whose submarine is it?

Mule Ship

Crew of Lifeboat #3, rescued by USS Rock (SS 274). Author is second from the right, back row. Missing is Chuck Kimmer. He was taken below to the sub's sick bay to have his badly ulcerated leg treated.

Dick Sproul

A discharge 'at sea' is not a good thing as payroll stops at discharge. These sailors waiting for rescue were eventually given 'Subsistence and Quarters.' pay

Selective Service cards which survived the sinking and weeks in an open lifeboat.

Mule Ship

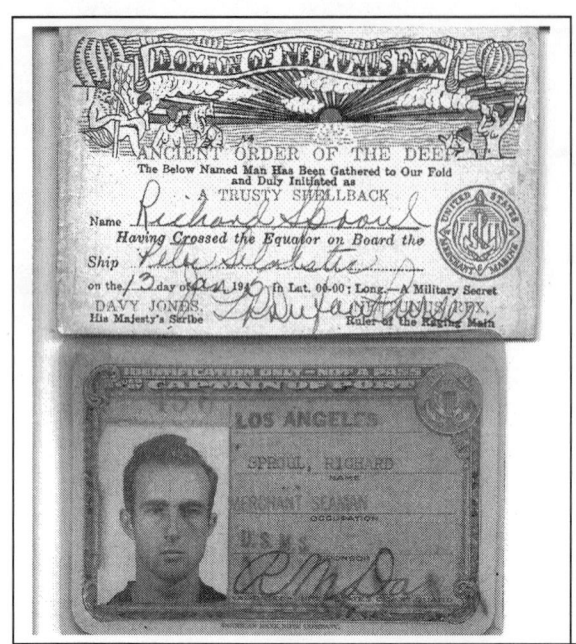

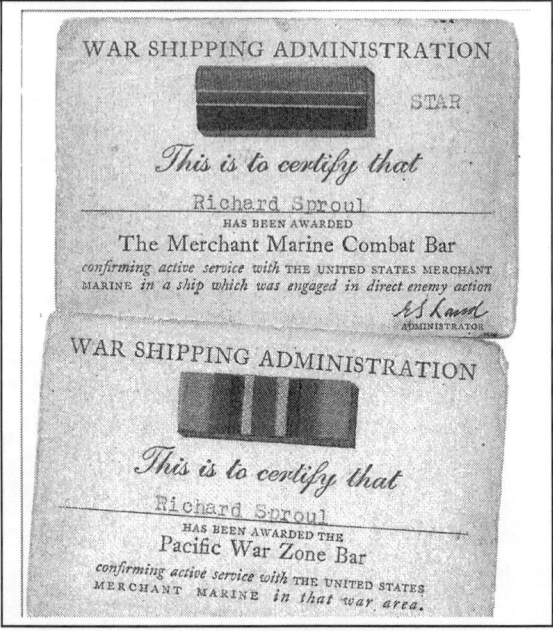

Other cards and mementos

Dick Sproul

Part IV

As each day takes forever to pass, it starts, most days, with the sun poking its fiery edge out of the sea then the sun and time slows, taking a lifetime to finally complete the day and sink yet again back into the Indian Ocean. And another long empty night follows. Day after day, some incredibly calm, with bright sun, others rough, windy with dark skies and menacing clouds scudding above us, but no ships or planes, or more hopeful, land.

Fear takes the place of conversation, not that there was any overly talkative guys in this boat anyway. In another place and a different time I might be appreciating the scene, Skies and sea constantly changing, heaving mountains of water and white caps or soft, smooth swells raising our boat then lowering, eight or ten feet. Sometimes threatening wind or no wind at all. But the crawling in my stomach, the unknown, prevents anything but tightness.

I continue to worry about my mother worrying about me. I keep trying to think of other things. Thoughts of friends. Guys in the neighborhood. What would they think if they knew where I was right now? Or do they know? Has our missing ship been reported. I wonder where they all are now? Again my thoughts travel back-

I had grown up on 78th Street in Los Angeles. I think I was three when we moved there after living in a duplex my

Mule Ship

grandparents owned in Los Angeles. Technically, East 78th was Los Angeles County. Central Avenue at the end of our block was the city limits. That was the way LA was laid out. The major portion of the city encompassed the area from Pasadena to Santa Monica, parts of San Fernando Valley and then a narrow stretch of land reaching out, connecting San Pedro and the harbor. It was that stretch of land that was a half a block away.

It was the kind of neighborhood zoned for single family houses on the north side while the other side of the street commercial property was allowed. This because the next street over was Nadue Avenue, considered a thoroughfare, is zoned "Commercial." The "Lumber Mill" and the "Putty Factory" as we called them, each occupied about four residential lots to span between the two streets. With brother Gene, we would stand by the large open doors watching the men work. Fascinated by the whirling machines powered by wide leather belts connected to a long shaft bracketed to the wall. We often made the lumber mill our stop during our neighborhood patrols.

"Don't go too far. I want you to hear me when I call you for lunch!" my mother's command ringing in our ears.

The shaft, itself, was powered by the largest electric motor I had ever seen. Each craftsman controlled his machine by shoving a long lever, guiding the belt to an idler pulley and back again to start and stop. The flapping belts, the lathes, the milling machines the shapers and sanders, and the men, did their wonderful ballet to add to stacks of doors, window frames, and porch rails.

The wood floor of the shop was interrupted by a slab of cement on which rested a large furnace into which wheelbarrows of wood chips and shavings were periodically dumped. In the center of this almost two-story building was a mezzanine housing the offices and probably a bathroom as there didn't seem to be one on the ground floor.

Dick Sproul

One day everything stopped, the door padlocked. It was the year I started First Grade, 1932, The Putty Factory, "Hunts Putty" somehow kept going but where there were four men working, now, most of the time there was only one.

The Emory's owned the gas station on Central Ave. Two glass cylinders on top of bright red pedestals with the "Gilmore" lion logo on the sides were sitting just inside the red tiled overhang. Inside the glass was a rod with small metal flags attached and numbered to show the gallons. With me in the back seat Dad would pull in the Model T and flip out the front seat cushion exposing the gas tank. Mr. Emory, it was always 'Mister,' would insert the gas nozzle and watch the gas level drop to the number of gallons requested. After payment, 16 cents a gallon, dad would replace the seat while Mr. Emory would pump the handle attached to the pedestal and re-fill the glass. Something about that bubbling gas fascinated me.

They also owned the property to the corner of 78th Street and Central. In the early thirty's they built a miniature golf course there. When that fad faded a small restaurant with a lunch counter was built. Finally they tore that down and built a two story stucco building--about 1939--where Mrs. Emory, who was the "business minded" of the couple, opened her real estate office above the restaurant.

Mule Ship

The Neighborhood Hero

A year later we moved up the street, past the empty lots, into the small one bedroom house behind a new stucco house on East 78th Street. The market crash in 29 hadn't affected the West Coast yet so Dad was still working in Los Angeles at Rocky Mountain Steel Products where they made rear axle and brake assemblies for Model T Fords. We had been living in a rented house just down the street and Dad learned that the fellow that had built the house had shot himself and the property was in foreclosure. The "old Canuck", as Dad called him, had apparently lost his money in the stock market when he decided to pull the trigger. It must have been tough on my mom crammed into that house with two small kids. I had my fifth birthday there. The five room stucco house was rented to a lady and her little blond daughter. She was about my age and her mother would frequently take her over to Hollywood hoping to get her into the movies. That was the story but it wasn't long before they moved out and we moved in and rented out the smaller house.

With his machinist's skills, Dad was always able to find work throughout the Depression, except for about three months in 1934 when he worked on the WPA. Then he got a job with the Hughes Tool Co. owned by the young Howard Hughes.
There were empty lots on both sides of our house when we first moved in, but about a year later a three bedroom bungalow style house came down the street on large house-moving equipment and carefully settled on a

Dick Sproul

foundation that had only been poured a few days earlier. The Dobbins family moved right in.

Of course my brother Gene and I were disappointed when we learned that their only boy was not a kid. Then another house, a big old Victorian style place was moved onto the fourth lot to the East and quickly occupied. The Parquet family did have two boys. Nick, about my brother, Gene's age and Johnny a couple of years older. It wasn't long before our front lawn and the two empty lots next door became a gathering place for several neighborhood boys.

Dad took pride in that lawn but still didn't seem to mind when we played on it. Of course when the gang got too large we always played in the lots next door. Grass, or weeds, never got a chance in the middle of those lots. But that too is another story to think about.

We had a game we called "sidewalk tag". The rule was you could not touch the sidewalk and had to jump from the parkway lawn to the driveway strip and back to the parkway. One Saturday this game was well underway. I was being chased by the "it" guy and laughing so hard I fell down. But then strangely I could not get up. Every time I tried I fell down again, laughing even more at this situation. A strange screeching sound and a low rumble filled the air.

All was quiet very quiet. Nobody was laughing. A loud thump got our attention. A large vent pipe on the roof of the abandoned factory across the street had broken loose and was rolling down towards the row of joined one-room apartments we called The Courts. Just as the pipe hit the side of the building four of the apartment doors opened all at once and a lady bolted out of each door. This slapstick scene started another round of laughing.

I heard the side door slam. My mother appeared with a frightened look on her face. "Are you boys all right?" Why would we not be all right I wondered?

"My God, that was an earthquake!" she said. What's an earthquake? I wondered some more.

Mule Ship

Dad came running from the back yard. "Jesus! I thought the Dobbins' house was going to hit our house. It moved three feet our way and then bounced right back the other way." Our house appeared to be unscathed.

We all moved over that way to see the Dobbins' house, which was set back further than our house and had been out of our view. There it was, like a beached whale, each end of the frame house now flat on the ground, the middle still held up by something. The heavy front porch railings had pulled apart and exposed large shiny nails. This, I thought, explained the screeching sound. The front door was wide open and we could see the linoleum floor humped up in a huge arc. I noticed the stucco side of our house now had a crack from the ground to the roof. None of the other houses we could see from our house seemed to be affected. Standing there in awe with other neighbors that had gathered we heard a hissing sound. Then someone said "gas!" Most of them started to move back. Dad stepped forward, hunkered down and looked through the shattered crawl space door. I followed him.

"Get back!" he ordered, "The meter's OK. In fact I think its holding up the house. Its the outlet pipe that's broken. I'll get a wrench." He took off, headed for our garage.

"I wouldn't go under there." From one of the neighbors. "That place could collapse any minute!"

"Gas is leaking out and my house is too damn close!" dad yelled back.

Holding a large wrench, dad quickly returned. "Dick, I told you to get back!" he said. He got down on his belly and wiggling under the house, only his feet visible. Not moving an inch, I stood there, petrified. What if the house did fall on Dad?

The hissing stopped. Dad crawled back out, dusty and a bit of a smile on his face. "It's safe now unless we

Dick Sproul

have another shake. Those gas meters must be pretty strong."

"Sproul, you got guts." Again from one of the neighbors. I couldn't have been prouder.

That night, we slept out on the front lawn under blankets. There were a few after-shocks but nothing like the first one. The Dobbins family, apparently not home that day, never returned. I wonder what happened to them?

It wasn't but a few days when a crew arrived early in the morning, jacked up the house and re-set it on the foundation, hopefully with better bracing. In a few weeks it looked as good as ever and the Cramer family moved in. One boy, Buddy, my brother's age and two older sisters, Kathryn and Clara. I remember thinking how pretty Kathryn was.

Buddy and Gene soon became pals and would go off together but that was OK, the empty lot was there and becoming the gathering place.

Mule Ship

A Windy Day, The Little Blimp that Could

I thought about how our neighborhood in Los Angeles in the 1930s was unique. Unique, not only in its ethnic diversity of families but also rich in range of experiences. Besides the empty lots, which stayed empty all through the depression and became our private playgrounds, there was the putty factory down the street from my house where I could walk in and watch the mixing machines blending the oil and powdered clay into putty or sometimes modeling clay. The big blond muscular fellow, at times during the depression the only fellow, would sometimes reach in and toss me a handful. He knew I would use it to mold something and not throw it around like other kids had done. I had brought in some of my "masterpieces" to show him.

There were other events that fascinated us all. Like the WPA project installing a huge storm drain down Hooper Ave. Even during the Depression California was still growing. And just two blocks over, were the truck gardens (small farms) run by a couple of Japanese families. The kids all used the term "Jap Gardens". This was the 1930's. But the one thing, right in our neighborhood that only one other city in the country had, was the Goodyear blimp. Akron Ohio, home of the Goodyear Tire and Rubber Company was the only other city with a blimp in the nineteen thirties.

Most every clear and sunny day, after spending the day cruising over the beaches or other parts of the county where people might congregate, the blimp would come home to roost at it's huge hanger at the Goodyear factory not far

Dick Sproul

from our house. The prevailing wind out of the west dictated the landing flight pattern bringing this bulbous silver airship right over our house each evening. Goodyear Tires in large dark blue letters emblazoned on each side.

At the corner of Central Ave, at the end of our block, and Florence Ave, just six blocks east, stood the mammoth factory that made tires for the entire western part of the country. Four or five acres at the south end of the huge complex were cleared for the blimp landing field.

As soon as we spotted the approaching airship we would often run or ride our bikes up Central Ave to watch the blimp land. In the middle of the open space, waiting for the arriving ship, were always five or six men and a gray panel Dodge truck with a pointed pylon attached to its top.

As the blimp came around in it's landing pattern, nose now pointing up-wind, just clearing the power and telephone lines lining Central Avenue, it would tilt downward, throttle back it's engines and move slowly up to the pylon. The men on the ground would grasp four trailing ground-handling lines to guide it's final movement. Some kind of latch at the peak of the pylon would engage the metal eye on the blunt point of the blimp's nose. Now secured, engines stopped, the blimp would obediently follow the truck over to and into the open maw of the corrugated metal hanger. Always a fascinating ritual to any young boys around.

Then one fall day a strange and sudden wind came up. Still right out of the west but much stronger than I had ever seen. Thirty, forty or more miles per hour. "This is a hurricane" someone decided. We had just seen the movie "Hurricane" with Jon Hall and Dorothy Lamore so we knew what a hurricane looked like. We experimented to see how far we could lean into it and not fall down. Then we got on our bikes and found that by holding out our coats we could sail down the street without pedaling. Of course pedaling against it was impossible, so with much effort we pushed the

Mule Ship

bikes back home. It was probably after a half-hour of this new kind of activity when someone saw the blimp, at first a small speck at great distance off to the west rapidly growing in size, hurtling toward us. The pilot started his turn early in an effort to compensate for the wind. A bit late in making that turn he found himself now a half a block or more downwind of the field. His two engines now roaring, the craft struggled to make headway. In fact the blimp was going nowhere. Stationary, as was the blimp, we were transfixed. How could the blimp land?

We all took off at once, running; as best we could against the formidable resistance of the wind, up the street to Central Avenue where we would be able to get a better view of the impending contest. What would happen? Would the blimp run out of gas? Where would it end up, in Riverside? Maybe it will be blown clear to Arizona!

But then, so very slowly, the blimp inched forward. The two radial engines, just like the one Lindberg had on his Spirit of St. Louis, straining to push the inflated craft. Ten minutes, twenty, inching over Central Avenue with traffic and street cars moving along below. Then just as the nose crossed over the field fence the movement stopped. Either the wind had increased or the engines were loosing power.

We moved north up the avenue now leaning sideways against the force. Other people were coming out of the stores and buildings to watch. Closer, the engine noise now louder, we saw the landing crew standing helpless on the field.

Another ten minutes went by. Was it moving? ----Yes, the small cabin at the bottom of the blimp was now over the field fence! Then it lost ground, Moving backwards the nose now right above the fence! Another ten minutes passed. Now gaining! Back to where it was! Still, it had another forty feet to go before the tail would clear the telephone poles and the chain link fence. How could he have any gas left? The wind felt as strong as ever. We stood there in awe, amazed at what could turn out to be a really bad day for our fat friend. If even one of those engines were to burp the blimp would quickly be blown off into the distance.

Now inching ahead the two forward handling lines finally came into reach.

The ground crew quickly leaped up to grasp the ropes, two men to a line. Holding tightly they added their effort to the laboring engines. After a minute or two of frantic effort the blimp was connected to the truck which now seemed way too small for the job. This time the pilot continued to apply engine power, obviously to prevent the truck from being dragged backwards. The propeller blades whirling perilously close to the ground and also to the men trying to save her. Quickly all of the men piled into the truck adding their weight. The assembly now moved slowly towards the hanger.

Just as the blimp approached the hanger it started to wobble a bit, the strong steady wind now turbulent as it passed around the structure. The men scrambled out and again grabbed the handling lines, fighting to steady it. The blimp, engines now cut, was moved hurriedly into the hanger with only a slight bump or two against the sides of the large opening.

Our blimp was safely home.

There was another time our sky was filled with a silver ship. Noon recess at 79th Street School and under white billowing clouds, the playground filled with noisy kids, it was a typical California day.

At first it was only a faint distant hum like buzzing bees, then growing louder and louder still. One by one the kids stopped to listen. Soon the playground was quiet, only the growing sound coming from the clouds, now a vibrant roar, seeming to shake the very earth. All eyes raised, now fixed on the clouds, wonder and a little fear perhaps, showing in those eyes. Nothing moved.

Mule Ship

But then one of the white shining clouds started changing into something different, smoother, shinier, it bulged out over us, wonderful, magical.

The magnificent United States Navy airship Macon stretched out over us, only 3 or 4 thousand feet up. The gondola with the crew looking out at us, the engines, four hanging from struts on each side, propellers whirling. I had only seen it in newsreels at the movies, along with its sister ship the Akron. Here it was, for real! Gliding right over our heads. Finally the tail fins emerged from the cloud, then it was gone, faded into the distance, and all was silent for a minute.

The bell rang and the now, very excited kids, surged back to class.

It was only two weeks later that newspapers headlined that the U.S. Navy airship Macon broke up in a wind storm off the coast of California on its way back to Moffett Field on the return trip from San Diego. Only one of the crew was lost. All others were saved. That signaled the end of the Navy's experiment with large helium filled Dirigidiibles.

Then the war and soon there were blimps everywhere, on both coasts, patrolling for submarines.

Dick Sproul

The Wind in Our Sails

The wind against our small sail has driven us east but also north. Hundreds of miles are now behind us. Our food is gone and our water will last only a few more days. Did we make a wrong decision to go for help? The men on those rafts must have surely perished by now. Sleep for me seems impossible. A bone-deep weariness drains the strength from me. But I resist, I fight back, I have to! I will prevail! We will survive! I am determined to get through this.

The Lords Prayer is invoked over and over again. The 23rd Psalm pushes the fear back down, momentarily subduing it. But the fear won't die, it is only dormant. When again the longed-for sleep seems so close, just as the drowsiness brings a chance to sleep and renew my strength, the fear comes back. It is there, like some poisonous snake in front of my face, coiled, motionless, ready to strike, but there, still there.

It explodes in me again! This new surge of fear snaps me awake. The fight resumes. I cannot give up. I will not give up. The drowsiness is gone, the weariness remains. I start yet again thinking of home--------

Mule Ship

*S*till in Edison Jr. High School I started working at Pratt's Coffee Shop, washing windows, moping floors and sometimes washing dishes. After awhile Rex, the owner, let me run the candy counter during Saturday Matinees. One day after I had worked there a few weeks Rex took me aside.

"You know if you get hungry or thirsty you can make yourself a malt or a sundae." Wow! I had watched the counter girls make those for the customers but hadn't dared to think of just getting my own. A new appreciation for this job set in.

One of the first things I purchased with my earnings was a new bike from Pep Boy's Auto store. A balloon tire beauty, cream colored with blue trim. It had a tear-drop shaped head light on the front fender and a luggage rack on the back. With great pride I rode it around to show all my friends. And then--- taking away some of the glow--- I found the words "Made in Japan" stamped into the metal under the pedal crank. It did however, in spite of the reputation of Japanese products, turn out to be a very sturdy bike. With my buddy, Mike Rizzi, perched on the rack, we ranged over all of southeast Los Angeles. When I would get tired Mike would stretch his legs forward and take over the pedaling. Most of the time we would ride on the sidewalks or on the left side of the street. The idea of cars coming up behind me was something that made me nervous. I had decided that seeing the driver's eyes was necessary for survival in the LA traffic. When we encountered pedestrians (or saw a police car) we would zip into the street or simply stop and quickly hop off and start pushing the bike until all was clear.

When our course took us up over a curb I would yank up on the handlebars lifting the front wheel up over the curb. Then I would lean forward putting most of my weight on the front wheel while Mike would put his feet down, taking his weight off, then with a hop resume his place on the rack just

Dick Sproul

as the rear wheel rolled up and over the curb. We had this routine down so that we could do this almost without slowing down. We were both growing—fast .I had grown a foot taller and added 35 pounds since starting Edison Jr. High School. Mike was even huskier.

Then the inevitable. Somehow our timing was off. The rear wheel struck the curb with mike's full weight still on the rack. With a pop and a twang some of the spokes just gave up. The wheel twisted like a Mobius loop. We had to lift up the rear wheel and push the bike all the way home.

It took me week with a spoke wrench and some new spokes to get the wheel so it would clear the frame. It was however never to run perfectly true again.

Then Mike got a bike of his own. We turned 14 that year and I had spent the summer at my cousin's ranch in Oregon. When I returned we started high school and got jobs delivering the South Side Bulletin, a local free paper that carried advertisements of nearby stores and businesses. Bundles of the papers would have been dropped off on a corner where we would pick them up at 5:30 in the morning. Canvas saddlebags draped over the bike rack and another similar bag over our shoulders held the papers for our routes. After we got familiar with the routes I often slept in until six or six thirty and still finished the route in time to get home, grab some breakfast and get to school on time.

One winter morning it was misty and overcast. Up a bit late the night before I had a tough time getting up, but I did. Once I got the papers loaded I headed out, sleepy, eyes drooping. With gas rationing there was little traffic. Starting down Compton Avenue there was only one old car parked far ahead.

My chance to catch up on my sleep. Keeping one eye partly opened so I could see the curb slid by. With arms folded, that well trained bike drifting along --yes! I was sleeping yet seeing. Warm fuzziness engulfed me. Somehow the back of that old car, its naked spare tire rim came into vision, too late! The collision could not have been pretty. Simultaneously my jaw and the bike hit.

Looking around guilty and embarrassed I untangled myself. My jaw had glanced off the smooth curve at the top of the car, but the front fender was seriously wrinkled under the empty spare tire rim. I gathered myself, took another look to see if anyone had observed this debacle, pulled the fender away from the bike tire and continued on my way, assured that no one had seen me.

I wonder how many people have fallen asleep while riding a bike?

But now, here in this lifeboat, I can't sleep at all!

Now teenagers, in warm weather we would take off for South Side Park and the large swimming pool there. We would sometimes get into "horse water fights". Mike would hoist me onto his shoulders where we would challenge other guys--or better yet, a couple of girls--and splash water and push until someone would fall. I'm pretty sure we won most of those contests. Except when we were challenged by girls, we always "lost" those fights. I would fall with mock terror and make a great splash.

When the pool was cleared at the end of the day we would go into the dressing room and crank our bathing suits through the wringer, get dressed and head for home on our bikes.

I remember our trips to the South Side Pool began to include Mike's scheme to "cop a feel." Spying a couple of girls, especially well developed girls, standing in chest-high water and talking as girls do, Mike would take careful aim. With his arms stretched out in front of him and face down in the water he would kick smoothly towards them. If his aim was good and his open hands made contact ---which included a slight squeeze --- he would pop up and apologize

Dick Sproul

profusely. This tactic worked for him until that inevitable time when he got a roundhouse slap for his efforts.

A very red faced Mike looked around and when he saw everyone looking at him, and with me doubled up laughing, he realized that it was over. He could never get away with that again.

Then came high school--and Pearl Harbor. Mike got a job as usher at the Centro Theater and then urged me to apply. The previous ushers had been drafted and the manager was forced to hire us fifteen year olds. I had just turned fifteen in November.

"Tell anyone who asks that you are sixteen." he advised and fitted us out with spiffy uniforms. Short light-gray tuxedo-like jackets with shiny lapels and darker wool slacks with a narrow red stripe down the leg, pressed with the sharpest crease I had ever seen. A stiff white dickey and a black bow tie finished the outfit.

A new, very pleasant but immobilizing thing started to happen. Girls, pretty girls, older girls, even some who appeared to be adult women, often alone, stared and smiled, intense looks on their faces. This only happens in the movies. Red faced I would blurt out "this way please" and with my flashlight find them an empty seat.

I soon got over my embarrassment. Thank you Mike.

Finally sixteen we got our driver's license's. I had practiced for weeks in our driveway shifting gears, working the clutch, the gas pedal and the brake, smoothing the motions, imagining driving to different places, each stop sign observed, arm signals made, straight up for right turns, out for left turns, down for stop. When reaching my destination I would repeat each action and turn into our driveway—all without leaving that driveway.

War time gas rationing, however, severely limited our range. Drives to the mountains, trips to Tijuana and even checking out the Valley girls as the older guys talked

Mule Ship

about were no longer an option. I could borrow Gene's 32 Ford 3 window coupe or sometimes Dad's car but without gas coupons, actually a small book of stamps, black with a large "A" and each one good for four gallons. This was the ration allowed for each week for each car. With car-pooling there was sometimes a little left over that I could use. Of course there <u>was</u> the option of using the Street Car.

Dating girls, parties and trips to the beach interfered with our jobs that were a necessary evil needed to make money for; dating girls, parties and trips to the beach. Fremont High School--girls, cars, sports, dances, classes; in that order of importance, --was our life. And hanging out at Mel and Jene's malt shop over on the corner of Broadway and Manchester.

The term "Italian Stallion" hadn't been invented yet but thinking back it sure would have fit. We had both grown to an even six feet but Mike was more muscled than I. With a broad chest, good biceps and curly dark brown hair, combed long at the sides and a duck tail at the back he caught the eye of all the girls and even one female teacher. He was a good looking guy and he knew it. Still, a bit of uncertainty kept him from being overly conceited. All it took was for some girl to ignore him. He would act like he didn't care and then salvage his ego by saying he couldn't stand her.

Mike had started to smoke--Camels were his brand. I held off, mom's frequent lament; "They are habit forming" making me just fearful enough. And stubborn. Constant urging, "Go ahead have one."--be one of us.--was the implication. I never liked to get into something hard to get out of. That included "going steady."

Ha! What am I in now? I am in this lifeboat---maybe forever.

Dick Sproul

During summers and on warm weekends we'd bum rides or take the bus to Hermosa Beach, our high school hangout. Or sometimes just head over to the pool at South Side Park. I would go by his house and whistle. Mike would come out with a towel and Levis over his swim trunks. Mike's older brother Tony, would be practicing his guitar and I knew he would still be at it when we returned hours later. Up an down the scales, short little riffs, over and over. He was getting good at it, at least that's the way it sounded to me.

When I commented on it Mike would grumble "yeah, it drives me nuts". Then Tony was drafted and soon was playing with the Army Band at the Long Beach Army Air base.

Our routine at the beach would be; hit the surf first and the see if we could pick up some girls. Beach Bums to the core, we looked for girls that had brought lunches and then, if invited, "reluctantly" agree to share. Failing that, we would amble over to the "Pearl's Place" counter open to the beach-walk and get a perfectly toasted tuna sandwich. To die for, with tomato and lettuce, lots of mayo. Man, they were so good. ---Then back to school in the fall.

Gym class was over. Sixth Period gym was for the varsity workouts that continued for two hours after school was out. I was trying out for the football team and Mike was on the wrestling team. After a good workout on the field I had stripped off all my gear and stowed my helmet on the shelf just over my nameplate. With towel and soap I stepped into the shower room. There was Mike standing near a flowing showerhead. He was wet, his normally curly hair and long side burns were now plastered down almost over his eyes. Other guys were under showerheads and busy showering, not paying any attention to Mike. He had a bar of soap in his hand and was rubbing it around and over his crotch. When the lather was plentiful he began to spread it over the rest of his body. I grimaced and asked, "What the Hell are you doing? "

He grinned mischievously. "It's a good place to make lots of lather."

I gave him a disapproving quizzical look and he must have known what I was thinking.

"Oh no, I already washed my face. This is for just below the neck"

Oh sure, that was better? -----Anyway that was Mike.

Nineteen forty two, forty three and forty four, it was a great time-- for us. The rest of the world was in agony. But turning eighteen and registering for the Draft was in the future. Another time. Another life.

Reluctant to take my eyes off the horizon I return to still another endless day, to hope, to pray, to think. Maybe it's better to think about those days.

That empty lot, so many lessons learned. Not just ordinary things like how to build a camp fire and how to make sure it was put out properly, but lessons about sports. Not just how to play the game but about 'good sports' and bad sports. And about life. From the older kids we learned about sex, or thought we did. They were older so they had to be right. Right?

There were other lessons to be learned. At an earlier age and time that empty lot was our playground. Weeds wouldn't grow because of many small feet constantly playing football, baseball, shuffling around, choosing up sides for a game. If eight or ten guys gathered that was enough for two teams. Sometimes one of the older guys would simply say, "You, you and you are on my team," which would immediately raise protests. So we would fall back on a time honored "Einnie Meeny Miney Moe"----- and the teams

Dick Sproul

might be more balanced. Even so the score was often one sided.

One hot Saturday several gathered on our front lawn and we were horsing around wrestling on the grass or playing with Bizmark, my big old mongrel dog. A couple more guys showed up with an old football. It was beat-up but still holding air. The process of choosing up sides was delayed when we had to step aside the driveway for Aunt Ruth in her shiny 1928 Pontiac. The car was always immaculate, and Gene and I often heard the caution, "don't put your sticky fingers on the glass!" She got out and watched us, a small smile on her face. Always well dressed even in the distressing times of 1933 and of course with a stylish hat and a light jacket in spite of this warm day.

First, we had to pick team captains. Somehow Georgie started it off.

"Einnie Meeny Miney Moe, catch a Nigger by the toe, If he hollers let him go!"

Sudden movement caught my eye. The smile, now replaced with a firm look, as Aunt Ruth strode briskly toward us, "You shouldn't use that word!"

Puzzled, we all looked at her. "What word?" Georgie asked.

"That word. Colored people don't like that word."

"Well, that's what they are," Georgie defended, the first to grasp which word she was talking about.

"We are white people and they are black people and that word is an insult," she lectured. None of knew just what to say. We stood there assimilating this novel—to us-- idea.

That was my first discovery that Aunt Ruth, a skillful stenographer, was self-educated in many things. I didn't know then that she had joined the NAACP after learning of tragedies in the South, and wanted to "do something to support their cause." And in a later year it was from Aunt Ruth that I first heard about "How awful it was the way

Hitler was treating the Jews." It was because of her that my world started to become larger. She wouldn't have thought of herself that way but she was the first "intellectual" to have an impact on me and my brother----and the others too, I suspect.

Of course we still used the little rhyme for a while, perhaps out of habit, but a bit of guilt crept in and I remember we started using other ways of choosing teams.

That empty lot, so many lessons learned.

Thinking about that word, and other words often used to identify others, mostly those of a different race, different country, or just different, somehow they had become oddly overemphasized. I had always assumed they were just a way to make the story or comment more colorful. There were, a couple of times, when I heard, from what seemed to be an older southern white man, the word laced with emotion close to hate. But I guessed that people probably had their own reasons for that as did others when talking about anyone they had strong feelings about. After Pearl Harbor the word 'Jap' quickly changed from meaning merely a poor immigrant farmer, as in 'Jap gardens' to 'Those dirty Japs,' notwithstanding those well-liked Japanese students in high school, who soon had to leave for camps in the desert. Much to the dismay, and a bit of anger and frustration, of their friends.

Of course being a white Anglo-Saxon American---I guess that's what I am--- a certain pride existed; but surely this pride that I felt, existed in every group, didn't it?

So when people gathered to talk, neighbors, family or friends, usually just the men, the language was often 'colorful.' Other names for Italians, Germans, and Jews and of course Orientals were scattered in the conversations. German soldiers were 'Krouts', French and English soldiers

Dick Sproul

were 'Frogs' and 'Limeys'. The term 'Kike' applied to any sharp business man whom you thought took advantage of you, even though he wasn't Jewish. In California anyone from the northeast was a 'Yankee', not always in complimentary tones. I remember my Grandfather, who was from the "State of Maine" taking that, to me, puzzling tone.

Dad's brothers; I had four uncles; somehow lumped all Swedes, Norwegians, Germans, and even the people from Holland, as Dutchmen. 'That old Dutchman' or 'That big Dutchman' was often added to identify a character in the story. I did notice that the term was never used for women.

Never about hate; derision, ridicule or foolishness perhaps, but just as often about admiration or awe, depending on the action taken.

To me, growing up, this was the way it was. That is, until I met that football teammate on the short drive to the Rose Bowl.

Mule Ship

Still again, day after day, calm, too calm, then rough, windy, then calm again, slow smooth evidence of the sea's latent power, raising our boat up, we all scan the horizon, then down again while we face the slanted wall of each moving trough,----the summer sun turns the eastern horizon aflame starting it's interminable travel across the cloudless sky only to be eventually quenched into the sea 16 hours later. The eight hour summer night seems even longer on moonless nights. The Southern Cross on our starboard side giving small assurance that we are still on course. I'll take my watch at the tiller, if only I could rest till then.

When the moon does appear, up from behind the sharp black horizon the air is so clear, and reality changes---

At great velocity, at this very moment, am I hurtling towards it? So bright, so perfect. This wonderful tremendous object grows perceptibly larger each minute that I travel. My speed is close to a thousand miles an hour. If I were to stay this course I would crash to its surface, yet I know that my trajectory will soon curve away, sparing me that fate.

I am awed by the beauty of the image before me and the awareness of my travel through space. This is not a dream, nor is it fiction, it is actually happening.

My view tonight is through an incredibly clear un-obscured window with a dark rippled sill, illuminated only by reflected sunlight from that moon.

Space beyond is black, featureless, the moon's intensity overpowering all starlight.

I feel little motion as the small vessel I'm on moves with me. Or, I with it. It is quiet, calm; the only sound is the gently lapping of water a few inches away, the cool hard bench beneath me---reality changes back.

Dick Sproul

.

One Summer--A Different Time

Big billowing clouds and blue skies of a summer day-----so many memories begin that way.

*S*o much has happened---less than a year ago---on the sand at Hermosa Beach, the surf, the sun---I remembered-----.
 For us the war and the Draft are still a long way off. Mike and I, as required, had both registered for the Draft when we turned seventeen and a half, but since we both have birthdays in November when we will turn eighteen we don't have a care in the world. It's a hot day and we are off to the beach. Gas is rationed but I have a couple of gallons in the tank so no problem. Mike says something about meeting his cousin there. Some of the stories Mike had told me about Augie and the other Italian guys that Mike hung around with that were pretty wild and I didn't know whether to believe them or not. These guys sounded pretty rough.

 I park my 39 Ford, purchased with earnings working 50-60 hours a week, put the top up, lock the doors and we hit the sand. Hermosa Beach is our hangout as it is for most of the kids from Fremont High. We spot a couple of other guys we know and flip our towels down on the sand. The surf looks good but we are content to just soak up some sun.
 Mike drags out his pack of Camels and lights up. He offers the pack but I shake my head. We had been through this before, ever since Mike started smoking a year earlier and he had passed the point of being miffed because I didn't join in. I never revealed that, frankly, the term, smoking habit" scared me. That was the term my mother had used on

Mule Ship

occasion watching my dad light up. Mike was now doing a pack a day so I was beginning to feel that my fears were justified. The others joined him, smoking their own brands. I put down the vague feeling of being the odd man.

I had another concern. An unexplained reluctance of getting into things I couldn't get out of. The up coming Draft into the Army of course was the big concern. Another, more recent box-----that was the way I looked at it,---- was the high school practice of "going steady." The down side of that was the loss of a couple of girl friends that I was beginning to really like.

After three or four dates and I didn't get to the "steady" thing, well they apparently looked elsewhere.

It isn't long before Augie shows up with another guy in tow. Perhaps it was the other way around, Augie was in tow. His companion is definitely formidable looking. Probably in his mid-twenties, no taller than any of us, maybe even a little shorter but his impressive build and a military haircut identifies him before Augie introduces him. They both have on swim trunks and carry towels over their shoulders.

"Hi Mike," he ignores the rest of us, "This is my cousin Phil, he's a Marine just returned from Guadalcanal." Now we are really impressed and questions erupt about his experiences.

"You see any Japs?"

"How was it in the South Pacific?"

"Boy that was a real victory." And, "You guys sure showed them. Are you going back?".

The first counteroffensive of the war, the US Marine invasion of Guadalcanal had recently been just about the first good news since Pearl Harbor. For days newspaper headlines had carried this story. Both Life and Look Magazines had rushed out issues with grainy pictures of some of the destroyed Japanese forces. They also had the first pictures of dead Japanese soldiers.

Phil assures us he had indeed seen some Japs and gives short disturbing answers while we listen intently. He has a thirty-day Leave and is indeed going back.

"You guys should see the sack of gold teeth he has," Augie blurts out. "

Did you bring them?" This really gets our attention.

"They're in the car" Phil says.

"I'll get them" Augie says and Phil hands him the keys.

A moment later he returns holding a small leather sack. Phil takes the sack and pours out a dozen or so of what are indeed molars with large gold crowns attached. They lay there on the towel glistening in the California sun. There are still more in the sack.

Stunned, I consider the implications of what I am looking at. The war takes on a new meaning for me, and the others too I suspect.

"Wow." someone finally says. And then finally the question on everyone's mind.

"How did you get them out?"

"Did you use pliers?"

"No, mostly I used my rifle butt." Phil says very casually. Like it was something that anyone would do. This image too, is filled with still more implications. I have more questions but I am not about to ask them.

Finally, Phil scoops up the teeth, pours them back into the sack and tosses it back to Augie.. "Take them back to the car." We flop down on our towels.

It's quiet for awhile. I consider hitting the water. It is getting warmer and the idea of catching a good wave becomes even more appealing. Then as Augie ambles back to the street where the cars are parked he passes a gorgeous girl, a woman really, maybe in her late twenties or even thirty, walking across the sand. Short light-brown curly hair and wearing a two piece bathing suit that shows off a lot but still looks expensive. The latest fashion no doubt. She's a real knockout with a smooth walk that is very sexy. She's carrying a towel and a small beach chair. Augie turns checking out her backside. We all check out her front side. Phil too, is glancing her way.

Forgetting the surf I try not to stare and I do note the other guys are like me, glancing her way while trying make it seem they are not that interested. After all we are seventeen and think guys that slobber over a good looking girl are stupid.

Augie returns from the car, gives another look at the brunette who has now settled in her chair about twenty yards away and is rubbing lotion on her legs and arms. Up to now I have not seen her even glance our way. But as Phil stands up I think I see a quick look in our direction. Was that eye contact?

Phil takes off and hits the surf, takes a few strong strokes and plunges into the first wave. Abruptly he reverses his course and heads back to the beach.

Striding up to our group dripping water he reaches down grabs his towel, tosses it over his neck and without a word turns towards the lady.

Intent on working the lotion into her skin she seems startled when he walks up. Then she smiles and Phil drops down on his knees in the sand,

Intently watching this scene unfold we are now REALLY impressed. They talk for a few minutes. Still glistening wet he starts rubbing lotion on her back! Another twenty or thirty minutes goes by and it appears the conversation is going well. She's laughing. Phil, now sundried, stands up, walks over to us and says "You can take the car Augie, I wont need it." With that he walks back and waits a moment while she gathers up her towel and chair. They stroll off the beach together, her hand holding on to his arm.------

Dick Sproul

Six teenage boys stand there, their mouths open in awe, a mixture of awe, envy and fantasy showing in their eyes. Mine too, I'm sure.

In two different places, here in this boat always hoping, searching for something on the horizon, and on that beach not so long ago. My point of view of that day and Phil's Guadalcanal story having quite a different effect----------I wonder where he is now?

Other more trivial things came to mind. In the 1940's Fremont High and Washington High, built in the late twenties in booming Los Angeles, were rivals in sports and in other ways too. Both schools were notorious for playing pranks on the rival's campus. During one football season Fremont students arrived at school one morning to see a "W" burned in their lawn. Of course, Fremont responded by burning an "F" on the Washington lawn. The administration officials of both schools decided to discipline the students by canceling their up coming football game. This was hilarious to Manual Arts High School kids BECAUSE it wasn't a "W" on Fremont's lawn. It was an "M"!

Forgetting a moment I almost wanted to laugh, again. Here, on the other side of the world I wanted to laugh.

Mule Ship

One of the Good Guys

And not so trivial. Of course when you have a lot of time on your hands you think about a lot of things. Food of course if there's nothing to eat. Or family. You worry about them worrying about you. But sometimes you think about the kids from the neighborhood where you grew up. As a little kid there were others close to my age but the older guys were kind of heroes. Or at least those whom you respected and admired.

Among the many other European nationalities, German, Italian, Swedish, on our street there were two Jewish families. And by pure coincidence, really, they lived next door to each other. Beyond that they had little in common. The Budinskis had three daughters quite far apart in age with Edith being the youngest. At that she was still a couple years older that I was. Their dad at first eked out a living in 1930 and 31 collecting junk using a horse drawn wagon no less. We only learned this when he came down our street one day, calling out "old clothes, bottles,--- buy your old clothes and bottles" in a noticeable accent while the horse plodded along, the reins slack.

Edith and her sisters were horrified when he did this and that was the only time we ever saw him except occasionally in the evenings walking home. Their home was a small bungalow in need of paint set in the back of the 130-foot lot. The front yard was adorned with the largest pepper tree I have ever seen before or since. It had been there since this was open farmland. A great place to climb up and hide, be invisable. On of the main branches exited only a couple of feet above the ground and then traveled almost horizontally

Dick Sproul

before curving upwards at a shallow angle. A wonderful place to lay with my arms hanging down. I could imagine that I was a great leopard waiting for his prey. Or a cowboy, astride the branch riding into the wind on a hot summer day.

Next door was the Berkowitz family. Two boys and their mother. No father in evidence. At least I never met him. Their darkly painted two story house was larger and older. Probably moved to the site, as were several others that eventually filled most of the empty lots on the street. Jack, was the oldest boy and five or six years older than me. Oscar, the younger brother was a year or two younger than Jack. As brothers often do they had little in common. Jack, although dark as was his brother, was the golden boy. A good athlete, smart, polite and good looking to boot. Oscar, who grew to be a little taller than his older brother, had a long, heavy featured face and could be a bit belligerent at times. When we played ball in the empty lot it would be Oscar who would start the arguments, complaining that the call was wrong or about some other infraction that no one was sure of anyway. It was Jack who usually organized the football or baseball games and tried to be the arbiter. And it was Jack that captured my attention. He could build model airplanes. He crafted them carefully and with great patience. He had several Model Airplane magazines in his room that I read cover to cover. His attention to detail made the planes seem real. I would look over his shoulder observing every cut of balsa wood and glued joint. I bet I could do that!

After a few days the small finished craft would be taken out into the street, the rubber band wound tightly and launched. He showed me how he moved his arm straight out releasing the plane with its nose level or just slightly down.

"You don't want it to stall" he would warn. The plane had been built with a small twist in the rudder to offset the torque of the propeller. These facts he carefully explained would hopefully keep the plane going straight or

Mule Ship

at least cause it to curve into the empty lot across the street from his house.

It seemed however, that most of the time the craft would meet a sad fate. When it did turn into the lot, the wing would strike the ground and break off. When it went straight everything would seem fine and we would go chasing after it yelling what a great flight it was. But as it drifted one way or the other a parked car or a lamp pole would get in the way. Loud "oh no's" would signal the impending disaster. In either case Jack would pick up the wounded plane and patiently repair it for another attempt .And if the airplane did survive the first flight it would be quickly prepared for a second trip. I can't ever remember any two consecutive successful flights.

Then I started building my own airplanes. Jack would look them over and give a bit of advice on how to avoid problems. After awhile He stated that I did not need anymore advice. But I knew that. I just wanted his approval.

The years went by. Jack graduated from Fremont High School. Another year and it was summer, 1941. Jack came home looking grand in his Army uniform. Gold wings on his chest. He was a 2nd lieutenant. A pilot. I wasn't surprised. And then two years later he was home again. Now a captain! He was flying B-24s in the pacific. Tales of bombing runs over New Guinea. He described one mission. The early B-24's did not have a nose gun turret so the Jap fighters would attack low from the front to avoid the top turret guns. To meet this challenge Jack got the mechanics to bolt a 50-caliber machine gun on the side of the forward fuselage aimed straight forward. They carefully rigged up a gun site in the cockpit and had Jack taxi the bomber over to the gunnery range where they tested and bore-sighted the installation. Everything was perfect. All Jack had to do was line up the target in the site and bingo! He would be able to paint a small red rising-sun flag on the fuselage along with the symbols put there for each bomb run.

Dick Sproul

The next mission they encountered no fighters. And the next, no fighters!--then finally he had his chance! Over New Guinea again, here came a Jap fighter head-on, guns firing. The target moved right into the site. Jack had him lined up perfectly. He pressed the trigger. Nothing! He pressed it again. Still nothing. The Jap fighter veered off doing little damage. Jack heard the waist guns and the top turret firing. Jack looked down. He had not flipped the "ARM" switch!

It was during these years that my knowledge of everything about aviation grew. How airplanes flew. Things about lift and thrust, drag and gravity. Engines were made by Pratt and Whitney, Wright and Lycoming, Rolls Royce and Allison. California aircraft companies were Douglas and Lockheed. I cut out information coupons from Flying magazine with all the well known builders of smaller planes Beechcraft, Vultee, Piper and the sleek shiny Luscome, the first all metal light plane. Gene and I memorized every detail of air speed, range, type of engine and payload.

All of this I'm sure, helped me do well on that Air Corps test----------but what good is that doing me now?

Mule Ship

Still Heading East

As it has for so many times before, this night ends with the black star-punctured canopy giving way to light ever so slightly in the east. Then brighter and brighter until a pin point of fire appears, quickly stretching into a short strip as though the water itself had caught fire. Smoothly changing into a brilliant crescent, I had to look away. In just a moment, or so it seemed, the full orb of the sun would rest for an instant on the surface of the water before beginning it's upward travel . It's movement would seem to slow and then begin it's interminable progress across the cloudless sky. Another day.

Of course here we are, still heading east, --- I hope. I take this moment to wonder what my fate would be if I had been able to join the Army Air Corps. My eyes were just not quite sharp enough. All those aviation magazines I had eagerly studied. Flying magazine, Model Airplane News and of course Alexander P. deSeversky's book, Victory Through Air Power. deSeversky's book was a revelation about the fallacy of fixed fortifications and battleships. Air Power was the only way according to him and he made a compelling argument. One of his statements: "If you're headed in the wrong direction you can't get where you want to go by speeding up" -------I sure remembered that now.

Perhaps we are also going in the wrong direction. I knew that although our lifeboat was pointed east we were actually moving as much north as east.

With the mainsail pulled tight the boat would move much faster, but without a keel the wind, still out of the

Dick Sproul

south, was pushing us sideways as much as forward. When it was my turn at the tiller and no one was watching and especially at night, I would gradually slack off the mainsail and jib. The boat would heel back to level and slow but our wake would straighten out behind us. I knew we were now heading a true course. Much slower but truer.

Even knowing this I still opted for faster. We were running out of time. With only a small bit of our rations remaining my ribs were becoming more visible each day.

Tightening the mainsail and jib the boat would again heel over and our speed and direction would be as before. In the dim starlight I could just make out dark curls of our wake angling off behind and to starboard. My hope was that Australia is a big continent and we could not miss it. Or had we already? In that case our landfall would be the island of Java hundreds of miles further north and east. Is this the right direction? Am I doing the right thing?

Larson

I was tired. So tired. I wanted to sleep. Finished with my watch at the tiller I sat down on the bench next to the man I had relieved an hour earlier. It would be hours and well through the night before I worked my way up to the head of the line and reach the place where I could lean against the arch of the bow spray curtain as well as the side curtain. Supported in two directions it was possible to get relaxed. Sleep would surely come. As each change of the watch occurred every one would move over one space toward the coveted spot. But each night everyone leaned against the man on his right and some seemed to be able to sleep in this position. As the line of leaning bodies got longer the accumulated weight would increase making real sleep impossible for me. As my position changed I tried to stay upright so as to not add my weight to the line in an effort to make it easier on the man next to me. Finally in the dark early morning hours it was my turn to reach the coveted position next to the spray curtain. I optimistically settled in hoping for the treasured sleep. Even a few minutes would be treasured. As I finally start to dose off I feel the pressure of the apparently sleeping Kent, leaning on me, the rod of the spray curtain digging into me. I'd had enough.

Shoving Kent upright "get off me!"

Somehow Larson had moved in front of me. "You can't hit my friend." His fist connected with my jaw.

What the hell was this?

Dick Sproul

Now I'd been hit before and there was never any pain felt with the blow. Just surprise, and shock I guess. A couple of times I had done the hitting. In the sixth grade it had happened and then later when I was sixteen I hit my brother. It was a sucker punch triggered by what I perceived to be a taunt. It was a left hook that missed his jaw and struck his mouth pushing his two front teeth back a bit. My attack was totally uncalled for and triggered by something completely trivial. I immediately regretted it. But it was done, I couldn't take it back.

We were seated at the kitchen table eating the lunch mom had prepared for us. Gene insisted on reading the paper at the table with the edge of the paper toward my eyes. For some reason this bothered me and I slapped the paper down. He calmly replaced the paper. Again, with more force and some kind of comment I repeated my action. Gene again replaced the paper. This was too much. His seeming indifference to my action infuriated me. In frustration my left fist came around and the blow landed. Gene did nothing but place his hand over his mouth. Mom was horrified

"Why did you do that." Mom cried out. I mumbled excuses about the paper and how it bothered my eyes. Even at the time I realized how ridiculous and mean that was.

Back in the sixth grade the story was a little different. Each day at recess the kids would run out on the school playground to the volleyball nets and quickly get a game going. The net was hung between two yellow wooden poles. Each pole had a step placed so the school janitor could easily reach the top and tie the net. Of course doing this each weekday morning was accomplished quickly and it was easier to leave considerable sag.

Now, eleven-year olds can sometimes be mischievous. I was no exception. On this day I climbed up on to the step to observe. After a few volleys where the ball just cleared the net I decided to pull the net taut. The ball

Mule Ship

dropped down instead of going over the net. Loud cries of "Hey!" and "stop that!" At the next opportunity I did it again. Same result. This was fun! The players were becoming more agitated and openly hostile. Still I did not stop.

They finally had too much. The players gathered around the pole, red headed Macgregor in the lead. "You better stop that." I looked down at him. I was out of reach, so I thought. He grabbed my ankle and jerked my foot off the step. Down I went, stiff-legged. The jolt as I hit the ground did something strange to me. Completely out of character for me, I faced him, my fists clenched.

"You want to fight?" I blurted out.

"Yeah!" he said thrusting his face into mine. Without warning, even to me, my right fist came up slamming against his jaw. He stepped back, a small trickle of blood appeared from his lip. My God! What have I done! He is going to hit me back!

Saved by the bell! literally. Recess was over. I have escaped retribution----haven't I? I turn and head for the building. But now McGregor recovers and comes after me, his hand on his lip. I walk faster. Sticking out my arm I hold him off, his fists pummeling my arm and shoulder. It seems my arm is longer that his. He finally gives up this and I hasten to class.

"This isn't over!" I hear him say. With a quick glance back I see an angry, frustrated look on his freckled face. Now I have a new worry. Will he be waiting for me after school? But he is nowhere to be seen when I hustle off the school grounds and head for home. I am totally relieved.

The next day at the start of lunch time, McGregor finds me in the crowded hallway. "Hey, I 'm sorry about that thing yesterday" he says. He's apologizing to me? I'm completely mystified and embarrassed by this unexpected behavior and mumble something similar and slink away.

Dick Sproul

But in the eighth grade, Edison Junior High, it was different. I get mine. Mike and I had made plans to meet at the top of the school yard bleachers for lunch. It takes me awhile to get my lunch bag and get out to the schoolyard. The bleachers are now almost full of kids munching or talking. The painted wooden benches go up six levels, each one higher than the next. No railings at the back or on the sides.

I don't see Mike but I spy a couple of open spaces at top. Manuel Gonzales, in my Social Studies class but whom I barely know is alone in the middle. I carefully make my way up past the others seated on the lower benches already socializing.

"Hi," I say. "Can you slide over a bit? I've got a friend coming." He stares at me and in blur his fist connects with my jaw. I blink. I feel no pain but I am in total shock by this unexpected event.

"Why did you do that!" I manage to blurt out.

"None of your lip!" he snarls. Another blur and the fist hits me, again square on my jaw. Totally bewildered by this, I step back. The other kids are looking around, blank, concerned looks on their faces. . What should I do? There is no teacher in sight. If I hit him back what will happen? I'm in the eighth grade, kids get in trouble for fighting. Mr. Dryden had just talked about that in my Home Room class. Manuel is just sitting there glaring at me, fists clenched but not guarding his face, wide open. We are it the top of the bleachers, a six foot drop off the back.

I do nothing. Humiliation and embarrassment engulfs me. I step down and walk away feeling that everyone's eyes are on me. My eyes are wet. For a second I think about McGregor. Was this different? Only reversed?

Later when I meet up with Mike I say nothing. He explains that a teacher kept him in class for awhile to talk about a test that he had just taken. I know this is a phony excuse, he was probably acting up in class. I never see

Mule Ship

Manuel after that. Not after school, not ever, he simply disappeared. I still wonder what happened to him.

Larson stood there, straddling the cross seat, dim moonlight illuminating his determined face. I don't feel a thing. His blow is weak, ineffective. Behind him just below the gunnel of the tilted boat dark moving water awaits. Nobody moves. A silent minute passes. Slowly I begin to see where this could lead. I am conflicted, not sure what I am expected to do.

Finally Eieslstien says gruffly "Sit down Larson!" I am thankful for that, I don't have to retaliate.

After a moment I get up and move over to the lee side and lay down on the empty bench. With my weight the boat heels over even more. The water now rushing closer to the top of the gunnel, and my ear. I'm comfortable now but still cannot sleep. I so much want to. To forget about where I am.

Too late I see a bit of humor in this. I want to ask Larson if he hurt his fist? And a chance to get one up on him. Better to let it go.

Dick Sproul

Shooting a Flare

*W*atching that flare arc into the night sky our hope that some ship over the horizon would see it was probably foolish. What could they do? Even if a ship had been notified to look for survivors in this area and that was a dim possibility, they could take no action at night, unless of course it was a navy combat ship. They too would have to be wary. It could always be some enemy trick. It might be that if seen by a ships lookout the captain would report it at their next port of call. What good would that do us, now?

We are more anxious everyday and those flares are just setting there in the locker doing us no good. It was a long shot but it seemed the right thing to do. We would save a couple for use if we did see something. That night we saw nothing---as in all the nights before.

This was our prison, maybe twenty feet long and about six feet wide. The view was good, most days. Incredible blue sky and few clouds but I had a quickening disinterest in this scenery. My major concern was the horizon. Each time our boat would travel to the top of each eight or ten foot ocean swell I found myself sweeping that horizon, south, east, north, straining to see some speck that would be a ship. A plane in the sky. To the east I wanted to see land, Australia.

The 25th Day

It's very dark, no moon and a light breeze. A gentle swell. I've been off my watch for about four hours huddled under the boat cover trying to sleep. And then Tschirhart started to grunt faintly at first and then it would build, into a wrenching sound like he's done before. More often now. Like he is being punched in the stomach.

"He's got the convulsions again, come on Tom can't you stop that"

"I've tried. It just happens" he seemed to gasp and then, "grunt!" again.

"Maybe a couple of malted milk tablets would help" I suggested. We still had a few left.

"Yea. Anything to quiet him down" someone else chimed in. I heard the rustle of the boat cover as an arm reached out and removed the cover of the food locker. After bit of fumbling around in the dark I heard a yell.

"Jesus Christ, what are you doing!" a pause and then "He's got the damn hatchet. Put that thing down!" At that we whipped the cover off to see what was happening.

"He was going to chop my arm off" screamed Dufour.

Reaching out of his little bow apartment was the old Chief Engineer, the hatchet in his hand. "He was stealing food!" he croaked.

Two or three quickly reached out and disarmed the now bewildered old man.

"It's OK Chief" was yelled in his ear. "He was getting something for Tschrhart's stomach. He's having convulsions"

Dick Sproul

We weren't sure that the Chief understood what it was all about but he withdrew into his cover in a huff, whipped the blanket around himself, no longer looking at us.

The next morning when the Chief wasn't looking we removed the hatchet from its storage clip in the bow.

The next day would prove to be our greatest test.

Now our 26th day in this lifeboat, sails full, we are moving fast but perhaps still sideways as much as forward. The brisk wind is still out of the south creating white caps clear to the horizon. Looking southeast I see a distant bird, a sea bird that soared with it's wings straight out, rarely flapping. We had seen them before. Tail feathers split like two-pronged fork. A solid cover of gray clouds that looked like moldy cottage cheese closed off the sky. A freshening wind stirred the sea into frothy whitecaps. The bird now coming straight at us.

But then it wasn't a bird. The bird somehow became a plane. A PBY patrol plane probably made right there near home in San Diego, California. Just like the one that zoomed over our ship in the Pacific. There is no doubt. I had assembled a wooden model of it in High School for the civil defense program for aircraft recognition.

"A plane!" I shout. "A plane!" Some of the others, following my gaze, give shouts.

By now what is clearly a US Navy plane passing over our heads, just under the heavy clouds but still very high. We grab the oars and start splashing the water around us, a fruitless gesture as the sea is already filled with whitecaps. "Get the flare gun". Larson, scrambling, fished it out of the locker, aimed it straight up towards the plane, cocked the hammer and squeezed the trigger. By now the plane was passing over us. Nothing happened.

The flare is a dud. We had one flare left. The gun is quickly cracked open and the last remaining flare inserted. It fired, arcing up after the now diminishing plane. The flare reached its apex and then fell into the sea. It too was faulty. The small chute did not open nor did the bright flare ignite. They don't see us, our boat lost in those whitecaps. We sit there, disappointment on each face. The plane seems to alter its course a bit. But then I see that no one is manning the tiller and it's our boat that is turning.

"Maybe they saw us and are radioing our position" is voiced. We all know this is not true.

Dick Sproul

Fear

Gradually that different kind of fear started to set in. It started days before. That bone-deep kind of fear. The fear of the uncertainty. It took awhile. We have seen nothing, no ships, no lights, only that one plane. Now not even any birds. Just empty horizon. Cockiness I felt having survived the *Silvester's* sinking fades. Silent prayers were said openly now. The Lords prayer, the 23rd Psalm. Those who were Catholic said the Rosary. Especially at night, "Hail Mary, mother of God, fruit of thy womb." over and over again. Swearing diminished and then disappeared altogether. When someone slipped and swore he was quickly admonished by the others. "If we are going to pray and expect God's help we cannot take his name in vain."

A meek "sorry" is quickly offered.

Fear----- I've learned in the past few weeks that there are at least three different kinds of fear. When the first two torpedoes hit our ship there was the fright of immediate danger. The racing pulse and frantic thought of what my next actions should be. Emergency drill steps we had been told about but hardly practiced. Quick decisions I must now make. Knowing a wrong decision might be my last. The first kind of fear.

Then the intense numbing fear an hour later when the enemy submarine surfaced less than 50 yards from our lifeboat. The silhouette of the sub, even in the darkness, seemed massive, white water cascading from its structure. Any second now the guns will start firing. The wave of fear immobilizes, but the mind races. Fear so massive, so overpowering, it takes extreme effort to hold to reality. I must think! I tense and prepare myself to dive into the water at the first flash of guns. It is my only hope. How far into the water will bullets go? I have a life jacket on, how can I get deep enough? Can I get it off soon enough?

But the guns are silent. Only the drumm drumm of the engines are heard circling in the darkness, finally fading into the distance. Will they come back?

The third fear, the worst fear of all. Somehow deeper, more penetrating than the others. It endures, day and night. It saps your vitality, your will. Harder to fight. As the days pass our situation becomes more desperate. All control has been taken from us. Why has there been no rescue? Why have we not reached Australia? Where are we? Sleep seems impossible. A bone deep weariness drains strength from me. Each time I think sleep is coming a new wave of fear is born---it explodes outward from my gut, courses through my body---out to my fingertips. This final fear is not sudden. It creeps into my soul. But I resist. I fight back, I have to! I will prevail! We will survive. I am determined to get through this.

I've got to get my mind on something else! Think about home. I will get back home! I just know it!

Dick Sproul

Part V

The Storm

*A*s this day makes it's transfer into night the clouds become darker. Their ominous undersides coming lower. Quickly the storm surrounds us. Choppy waves that had buffeted us all day now become larger. Then even larger again as the wind increases until we think they cannot get any bigger. But they do and build into mountains, leaning, threatening mountains. Now gigantic but at the same time being ripped apart as the top of each wave is sheared off and hurled through space until it is slammed into the next wave already missing it's top. Down in the trough this ton of water would sometimes be carried over our heads. Spray and wind and noise is now our world. We had furled our mainsail earlier and replaced the jib with the heavy canvas storm jib. This gives us some headway and the man on the tiller fights to bring us about so the bow will pierce each oncoming wave. For awhile this tactic works. Now the waves become more chaotic and come at us from every direction.

Our precious compass is removed from it's usual place on the aft bench and safely stowed. If we lose it now we are really lost. Not important now anyway since we have no way of controlling our direction. No way of telling if or when the boat is turning. No stars or moon to see. No point on the horizon for orientation. We cannot see the horizon anyway. Each wave raising or dropping our boat in ever increasing cycles and when in the trough a wall of water is all we can see. In the next instant we are lifted up and exposed to the jolting wind and the spray that feels like bird shot. It hurts!

The boat slams over dangerously but the jib and sturdy mast withstand this fierce attack. Could they again? We quickly lower the storm sail. We are now officially a cork. A very small cork in this out-of-control washing machine. A cork that I pray will stay right-side up.

Down in each dark trough we are momentarily protected. It's almost quiet. But then on top again, dim starlight filtering through the thick clouds, the terrifying force of the storm comes at us again. And again and again and again. The wind's roar overriding the crashing of the water then blending together into an even louder crescendo. Now back into the trough I stare at the wall of water in front of my face. For an instant I see that huge wall all around us ready to fall on us. It is like being at the bottom of some gigantic funnel. Above us I see a dark disk of clouds a bit lighter than the black wall that momentarily surrounds us. How can water stand so high?--if even for a second. More than three or four times the length of our boat.

Our boat is almost 20 feet long. In the next instant, miraculously, we are lifted up still again. This time that ton of wave top slams directly into us. I turn my face away and grab onto the seat. It hits the side like a cannon explosion, swamping the boat. Full of water we are in danger of capsizing.

"Bail! Bail! Bail!" Grabbing the bucket and piss cans and even our hands we all frantically scoop water over the side. Every man flails at this intrusion of ocean. The boat begins to rise again out of the water. We are OK. Do I really think we're OK? Hardly. A few moments later we are swamped again.

Hours pass while this assault continues. The terrifying wind and needle-like spray does not let up. When the timing is right a wave brings us up just as the top is blasted off. A cracking explosion of wind and water and we are swamped again. This is a beating on top of a beating. Four more times during this forever night the boat is swamped. Each time the desperation of survival takes over. Shouting "Bail! Bail." We do what we know we have to do, while each prays urgently to God. *"End this!, Please end this!"*. New strength comes to us physically and mentally--------I have to renew my determination each time. I will win! We will win! There is no option, no second choice. If this storm goes on forever, I will go on forever.

With the dawn the storm finally tires of pounding us. Those fearful mammoth waves soften and then return to smooth swells, seemingly a bit lighter. We have survived the 26th day. The 26th night! Our determination held. We all give tribute to the designers of this sturdy little boat. It has taken everything the sea could throw at us. We have taken everything the sea could throw at us.

We have endured! The food lockers are completely empty but we still have fifteen cans of water remaining in the other locker. The decision is made to cut the daily ration to a half a cup a day. Any less will do us no good at all. One can a day will be emptied and tossed overboard. Tomorrow there will be 14 cans left in the locker. We can last two more weeks. That will be it.

We have no idea where we are. How far off-course did the storm take us? Our heading is, as always, 90 degrees due west towards Australia. My hope is that it's still there. I am beginning to entertain the silly thought that somehow Australia has simply sunk into the ocean, never to be seen again.

Mule Ship

The Toll

*E*veryone, even Louie can now count their ribs with ease. He has lost the extra weight he was carrying and now looks trim. Sunken cheeks on the rest of us are camouflaged with four weeks growth of beard. Chuck Kemmer is the worst off. The constant rubbing of his oil stained denims has created blisters on his legs that have turned into ulcers. His left leg is now completely covered, the right leg, less affected, is still looking bad. Calloused skin on fingers and hands is peeling off and I see a couple of guys biting pieces off and swallowing it. Tschirhart continued to have periods of stomach convulsions.

    We had given him the last of the malted milk tablets which helped for awhile. There are complaints that he's preventing some from sleeping. Who can sleep? I know I can't sleep, even when it's quiet.

    Carl Pfieffer, a very quiet fellow, seems to be doing fine except for his right eye. Gradually getting more inflamed and oozing thick fluid. We had found an eye patch and medication in the boats medical kit. With the black patch and his stained cap this tall unobtrusive man now looked the bit of the pirate.

    Assessing my own condition I see that the sickness during the first three days,--- God, how long ago was that? Was it simply sea sickness or had I swallowed some of that oily water?---has put me at a disadvantage. I can feel my pelvic bones pushing into my skin wherever I sit. Whatever muscle I had there is gone. When the weather is calm I use my life jacket as a cushion.

    White pus pockets are forming beneath my fingernails and under the skin of my right forefinger. If this continues I'll surely lose that nail and maybe another. My left hand seems OK except for my left thumb nail. That nail has always been damaged and maybe it will come off and grow a new one. If that happens some good will come out of this whole thing. Weakness and lethargy is apparent in everyone. Strange, I don't seem to notice the hunger--first the stomach sickness---now the seemingly continuous adrenalin surge, if that's what it is, supplants everything. Somehow lethargy and adrenalin seem to exist at the same time.

Two blisters that appeared on my right ankle a few days ago have now grown into oozing ulcers like those on Chucks legs. One is getting quite large, almost nickel size. Another small blister is now felt on my left ankle. This is the area where end of the pant legs rub just above the sock.

Now 27 days since our ship was hit and in just one more day and we will equal Eddie Rickinbacker's 28 days spent in a life raft. For a minute I fantasize about this potential glory. Rickinbacker was an American hero. A famous flying Ace, he shot down a bunch of German planes in World War One. Then in 1943, while on a special mission for the United States, his plane went down in the Pacific. There were big headlines when he was lost and then again when he was found, still alive with five others. But they had caught fish with fishing gear stowed aboard the raft and frequent rain supplied them with a some water. They even caught a seagull and ate him. The story made headlines and the details made exciting reading. Unfortunately, for us there is seldom enough rain west of Australia and we have no fishing equipment.

But then we are not in a life raft, we are in a boat. A very sturdy unsinkable boat with sails. Wait a minute, I should be happy if we spot land right now. Or better yet rescued by a ship or seen by a plane. To hell with the glory! How could I even consider any thing else? And yet,

something about the idea appeals to me. I now harbor a small wish that our rescue will wait for another day.
    How stupid is that?

Dick Sproul

God's Reality

*W*e sit there each day each of us lost in our own thoughts, but eyes ever on the horizon. Thoughts of prayer. We had prayed together over and over, reading from the Bible. Protestant and Catholic. Prayed to God. But privately wondering where that God was. And slowly, incrementally, but undeniably, an awareness of the nature of God seemed to reveal itself. God was everywhere. Yes, I knew that. But the idea that God was within us, God was within me, seemed to be the greater truth. There was an unavoidable honesty in that. I should be praying, not to some distant entity, not to Him who would hopefully turn to listen, but to God within me.

Gradually, a sense of power, a sense of calm and serenity and even a sense of eternity spread into my very being. I could not, I would not die here on this vast rolling sea. We would travel through this ordeal safely. We would! We would see the coast of Australia. It was my show. I would direct its outcome. I was surely a part of God and was responsible for creating and sustaining the will to live. To survive. To seeing that God's will, and my will, are the same. Or more accurately, insisting on it.

Light!

And there it is, it really is. I stop breathing. Or do I just imagine I saw something? Another few seconds and another flash, a bit brighter this time. I'm not sure. It's still so faint. Lightening from a distant storm? Millions of stars in the crystal clear night sky that silhouette our sail and darkly illuminate the ocean surface, as well as our boat, makes that notion seem wrong.

And there again, I start counting, one-two-three-----seven-eight. There!

It is a light, not lighting! Could it actually be a beacon light? But I want to be sure. That Seaman's Handbook I had in my kit cautioned about this. I want it to be a light, it has to be a light! I reach over and tap Martinelli, huddled under the canvas like the others.

"What!" he responds with a little irritation and pops his head out. He has no trouble sleeping sitting up.

"Take a look, there" pointing ahead. Nothing.

"What" he repeats, with a little more irritation.

"A light!" he screams "a light, a light!" He yells. All heads pop out.

"Where?" several voices and then, "Yes, Yes!" All see it. After a minute, "It's a beacon light. I count eight seconds between flashes." Someone who had experience. Pfieffer perhaps? He's the old hand here. It wasn't the old engineer. I can't see him at the far end of the boat

The gentle breeze moves us toward it. Dead ahead. Have we sailed directly to the harbor at Freemantle? Maybe it's a lightship marking the harbor.

Dick Sproul

After an hour of gentle breeze and slow sailing the flash now becomes an intense diamond as the horizon drops away. Soon it's dawn and the light goes off but now we can see a small orange and white derrick with a small building attached, no doors or windows. The low. dry desolate coastline stretches off in each direction to the north and south.

Now maybe a mile or more offshore there are no wires, no roads that we can see. The very weak faint west wind stops. We wait. Mid-day the breeze returns but now in the opposite direction, coming straight off the land. We lower the sail but cannot stop the increasing distance. Our elation dwindles. Our daily half-cup of water is rationed out but today we make it a full cup. Surely another day and we can make it ashore. Talk of the structure containing a phone or even something to eat keeps our hopes up. We will break in if we have to. After awhile the low coastline disappears back behind the horizon. Only the very top of the derrick stays visible for awhile. Thirty one days since abandoning ship. Where are we? Warm, almost hot, dry and cloudless. Now into March and late summer in the southern hemisphere. There are no currents and we do not drift north or south of what is now our intense goal, the goal we have been seeking for 31 days. Some seem to doze off. I cannot. Whirling thoughts of what actions we will have to take once on that beach fills my mind.

Darkness and the flashing light comes back on. Who turned it on? Why do they not see us? The unwanted breeze stops and we are motionless an hour or more. A breath of air returns now as before, towards the east and quickly the sail is raised. The blinking light, staying directly east comes closer again, rising again off the horizon, agonizingly slow. A long night and no one sleeps.

At dawns light and we see that we are closer this morning, surely only a mile. Maybe less, but as before, the wind stops, the sea almost motionless.

Mule Ship

Forty feet below us the sandy ocean bottom can now be easily seen through the crystal clear water. After days of dark ocean this view lifts our spirits but we wonder if the fickle coastal wind is going to tease us forever, land, terra-firma, survival, just out of reach.

"We've got to row" I urge. I look at our group, skinny, weak but now with determined expressions. Can we even lift the oars?

Clumsily, two on each oar get the oarlocks inserted and take up positions. The lethargy falls away. A couple of feeble strokes and a small curl of water shows off the stern. I pull as hard as I can on each stroke. Can I keep this up? I know we are moving but can discern no change in the gap to the light tower. Soon some seem to be played out and others take their places.

As the intense sun begins still another run at the sky. I look away to south where that low brown coastline of what we hope is Australia, disappears over the horizon. I blink, a tiny black dot is there on the surface of the water, smaller than a period at the end of a sentence. Soon I notice others looking. We keep rowing, silent the desire to reach that beach now more important, that's the still the goal, The black dot seems stationary---for awhile. Finally a bit larger. We keep rowing, now all eyes are on the dot. The dot takes shape.

"It's a fishing boat. Its has a high prow and low fantail"

"Yeah, I think so too. They must see our red sail." There is absolutely no wind yet so we have not lowered it as we did yesterday.

The fishing boat becomes a submarine, moving fast toward us. With the sun at their back this dark ominous, shape moves quickly between us and the beach, slicing through the water, froth off its bow. Who's submarine is it?

Dick Sproul

Back-lighted by the bright sun I squint, and hope. Fifty yards away there are men on deck, guns pointed at us.

Now moving past us to the north it makes a fast menacing sharp turn and charges back, almost directly at us. Passing us twenty yards off it's starboard beam it seems to squat in the water as full reverse is applied.

"You guys want a ride?" in clear American English, is shouted out. By Captain Keating of the *USS Rock*, we were to learn. We quickly lower the sail and ship the oars.

"Are you from the *Silvester*?" He asks, his strong voice coming across the gap like he knows the answer. Our reply is loud and unanimous.

A heaving line is tossed and we are pulled over to the side of the sub.

Hands reach down and hands reach up and everyone scrambles to get aboard. My knee thunks against the smooth rounded hull as I am pulled aboard.

"When did you get sunk?" is his first question when all are aboard. "The date on the report I received is February 6." We confirm this. "That's over a month! The word is that you were lost." Well, that was true but not like you mean. "Three other boats and three or four rafts were picked up weeks ago. One of the boats wasn't found until ten days ago" he corrects himself. That must be the # 1 boat that started out with us!

By the time I turn to look all are now standing on the sturdy oak slats that make up the deck of the *Rock*. Our lifeboat is drifting away only the slim line still attached.

"We'll tow it back." Keating announces, "It's three hours to our base where we can drop you guys off." Slack is paid out so the boat will ride well aft of the sub. The water boils and the sub lurches ahead. The line goes taut and then snaps like string. Again the sub comes to an abrupt halt. "We'll have to sink it. We can't leave it as a navigational hazard."

Mule Ship

The two sailors manning the 20 mm and fifty caliber weapons swing their guns and aim. "Start firing" Keating orders. "No" I want to protest. But it's too late, the firing begins. The 20 mm punches fist sized holes, the 50 caliber holes are thumb sized. The air tanks have to be punctured before the boat will sink. All eyes are locked on the #3 boat from the Liberty Ship, *Peter Silvester* as it settles upright under the clear water toward the sandy ocean bottom. The top of the mast with its small triangle of red sail seems to hesitate before it too slips below the surface. No one has retrieved a single thing from this amazing boat that has served us so well. The subs engines again surge and the view of our boat disappears even though I was sure it had not quite yet reached the bottom and its final resting place.

Chuck Kemmer eases himself down on the deck and leans back against the steel conning tower. I turn to the Captain. "I think you should have someone look at his leg." I say, pulling up his pant leg a bit. Seeing the oozing sores Keating calls out to take him down to sick bay. Three sailors step forward to lift and carefully lower him down an open hatch into the sub.

As I stood there on the deck of the submarine I took a moment to think about what we had just been through. Perhaps this was something that I had to go through. A maturing process. A growing up process. A moving away from depending on others; my parents, teachers, authority, to knowing that from now on I was in charge. Still, learn from the mistakes of others but to also decide on where I was going---a deep lesson that every action had consequences.

It was unfair to the others of course but I could not help but feel a sense of personal victory--a sense that I had done it. I knew we could make it! From the middle of the Indian Ocean 750 miles from the coast of Australia! It was

Dick Sproul

MY doing--my certainty--behind the doubts a deep feeling that I, and the others, would survive!

As an eighteen year old I survived ! I can survive anything! Even a bit of "I'm indestructible" was in there.

"Guess you are kind of hungry. 'Pass the word to bring up something for these guys to eat," Keating shouts up to the crew on the conning tower. "The galley always has some soup or something ready." We all agree to that!

The low beige coastline off the port side slips by as we sit on the deck and gulp down the beef-rice soup. It's thin but maybe that's good. And oh so welcome!

I can't help but note how desolate it is. Even the Mojave desert has some vegetation! Here it's just light brown nothing. But after awhile there is something. At first just a blotch on the beach. Coming closer I see it's a small rusty ship, battered and broken, well above the water line with black blotches scattered on the ground on either side. "That's Pot-Shot" the Captain says. "We use it for a target when we check out our guns at the beginning of each patrol. Its been there for years. Pot-Shot is the unofficial code name for our base."

Mule Ship

Exmouth Gulf

Finally within the bay, brown bare land now on each side of us, we spot a navy ship a mile or two ahead. Soon we could make out a small tanker also up on the beach like the wreck at Pot Shot. Then two more submarines laying low alongside of the navy ship became visible.

The tanker had split in the middle and dark strips of oil blackened the sand on each side and down into the water.

"That's our sub tender, the *Cousal*," captain Keating continued, "And that tanker on the beach ended up where it is after the hurricane we had six days ago. Only down here in the southern hemisphere they call them typhoons. But we are still drawing fuel oil from it. Only one of it's tanks is leaking so there's still plenty left."

"So that was a hurricane." I said. "We went through a terrible storm six nights ago too!" I wanted to tell him more of what we experienced but he turned and spoke a command to some of the crewmen on deck. Getting closer now we could see two Quonset Huts, a small water tower, some large tents and other pieces of equipment further up on the land. Still no vegetation, just brown and tan sand and small rocks. Thirty or forty men were busy at tasks or watching us. The wreckage of a lookout tower lay nearby.

Captain Keating continued, "It's amazing you guys survived that storm. All of the subs headed for deep water before the storm but the tender rode it out with all four anchors out and keeping it's engines running. The tanker's two anchors just didn't hold. It's lucky we made out as good as we did. We had only a few injuries and one fatality. Too bad, he was the only Australian here. Our liaison with the Royal Australian Navy."

Tying up alongside the outboard sub, a gang plank was pushed out to connect us with the other subs. And after bidding our rescuers goodbye and very sincere thanks, we made our way over to the tender, holding fast to the guy lines with each shaky step. We were met by a couple of the ship's officers while being observed by several navy crewmen. By the looks on their faces it was plain that they were wondering who these bedraggled people were? Skinny, dirty with caked-on oil-stained clothes and faces, and a month's growth of beard we had to be a pathetic looking bunch. With his gray balding head the *Silvester's* Chief Engineer, way too old and frail to be here in this war zone was being assisted by a couple of seamen sent over from the *Cousal* to escort us aboard. Devito with thick curly black hair that had not been cut for several months, Tschirhart and Jimmy, the lieutenant, in pieces of army attire and the rest of us in various bits of civilian clothes or government issue dungarees and tee-shirts. Kent and Larson still had their P-coats. And finally little Martinelli, still in his pajamas almost black with oil, bringing up the rear.

The shock of it all now setting in no one had as yet much to say. We were safe and that was taking awhile to sink in. I turned back for one last look at the Rock. Having topped off its tanks our rescue "boat" was casting-off for the second time this day. To resume it's patrol in harm's way. I would have liked to have stepped directly off our life boat onto the beach at VLAMING HD Light NORTH WEST CAPE--to prove we had beaten the sea and in a way, the enemy, on our own--but perhaps it's better this way-----

When I arrived in Perth, Australia three days after our rescue I learned that the Captain's boat was picked up after only four days. We had been given wrong information about the emergency radio, it had been working after all. The other boat, number two, and the rafts were picked up several

Mule Ship

days later by a US Navy ship, the guys on the rafts suffering greatly. Why the Captain didn't round them up seems strange. I did learn that he was fearful of capsizing and wouldn't allow rigging the mast and sails!

The navy ship put men aboard the still floating aft portion of the *Silvester* and shot each mule. They hadn't been fed or watered for over a week. Standing off they sunk the *Silvester* with cannon fire.

With the sinking of our lifeboat, the *Peter Silvester* was no more.

Jack Funk was not among the survivors.

Dick Sproul

ABSTRACT FROM THE DECK LOG OF THE USS ROCK

  Original signed by J.K. Leggett
Saturday March 10, 1945

Underway (on surface) in accordance with COMTask Group 71.1 Op order 29-45 on course 031 deg T at standard speed on three main engines charging batteries on one main engine. 003 Completed battery charge. 0005 Standard speed on four main engines. 0206 land contact SJ radar Bearing 086 deg T range 39,650 yards. 0325 sighted VLAMING HEAD navigational light bearing 049.8 deg T. 0345 Changed course to 270 deg T. 0353 Changed course to 031 deg T.

  Original signed by J.V. Carbrous Ens.

Underway as before on course 031 deg T at standard speed on four main engines. 0542 changed course 090 deg T. 0550 sighted sailboat bearing 075 deg T. distance 8 miles. 0630 maneuvering to bring sailboat along side. 0640 picked up 15 men, survivors of SS Peter Silvester at latitude 21 deg 41.5 mins South longitude 114 deg 07.6 min East as

Mule Ship

follows: J.S. Eiselstine Lt. USA, Thomas Tachirhart Pvt. USA, Mario Martinelli Pvt. USA, Frank G Cappello Slc USN, Lawrence Casseli Slc USN, Charles Kimmer Pvt. USA, James Nausler USMS. Vito Garubo USMS, Richard Sproul USMS, Eugene Larson USMS, Jack Cox USMS, Kenneth Penn USMS, James Folden USMS, Louis Dufor USMS, Carl Peffier USMS. Carried C. Kimmer down to sick bay to treat infected leg. Sank lifeboat with 20 mm and 40 mm fire after trying to tow it. 070 changed course to 090 deg T changed speed to all ahead standard. 0709 changed course to 134 deg T. 0737 changed course to 193 deg T. 0750 mustered crew on stations. No absentees.

Original signed by L.C. Yeiech LT (jg)

Underway as before. Made daily inspections of magazines and smokeless powder samples. Conditions normal. 0854 maneuvering on various courses at various speeds proceeding through channel to moor along side USS Coucal. 0911 moored to starboard side of USS COUCEL. Exmouth Gulf Western Australia. 0930 transferred survivors (from SS Peter Silvester) to USS Coucel,

Original signed by J.V. Carrous Ens.

Dick Sproul

Moored as before. 1240 commenced receiving lub oil aboard ship. 1340 secured receiving lub oil aboard. Received 630 gallons symbol #9370 lubricating oil, USS ROCK underway.

Mule Ship

And Then What Happened To…?

Jack Berkowitz'----I never saw Jack or Oscar again after that. Oh Jack survived the war OK but by the time I came home Jack had left again. He had re-enlisted. He wanted to stay in the Air Corps, soon to become the United States Air force. I heard Oscar graduated from USC.

Mike Rizzi was always away on another voyage when I was home and I didn't see him again until after the war. Johnnie Cardozo attended USC on the GI Bill and graduated with a mechanical engineering degree which amazed me. He was smart enough but if ever anyone had less mechanical aptitude than Johnnie I never met him. Most of the others went separate ways after the war and except an occasional meeting at high school reunions. My brother Gene, became an attorney and lives in Sacramento, California.

When signing up for my next ship I spotted Leonard the cook behind the counter at the Union Hall. He was conversing with two other ominous looking Union officials and I regret not confronting him about leaving the ship in Melbourne. Still eighteen, I guess I really didn't want to know. The implications of the question I wanted to ask where too great.

That ship, the *S.S. John Goode* was another Liberty ship but also converted, it was now a tanker. Fitted with fake cargo booms to fool enemy subs looking for tankers, the greater prize. Leaving on July 6th 1945, its destination I learned; Hawaii with a cargo of bunker oil. Off-loading at Pearl Harbor We glimpsed the sunken battleships under the

Dick Sproul

clear water, still seeping oil into the harbor. I found our return cargo unbelievable, thick, brown, bubbling, gooey unrefined molasses. All five of the ship's holds, now tanks, filled with molasses. I tried not to think about swimming in that stuff if torpedoed again.

During my shore leave after that trip the Atom bombs were dropped on Japan.

Years went by. Eventually I settled down and got married. Went to aviation school, got my license to work on airplanes. Became what we called --jokingly--an Itinerant Aerospace Worker. Took more night school classes.

Finally started working at Aerojet-General in Downy California.

One day they hired a rather short dapper gray haired fellow with a well trimmed, just as gray, mustache. Said his name was "Pappy" Parker. He had retired from the Air Force. We became good friends. He was no longer married so we had him over for dinner a time or two. He had a twenty two-foot boat and we were invited to go sailing with him. One time he brought some photographs. Some taken years before. One picture, a group of men in front of a new bomber was taken at Edwards Air Force Base. I couldn't believe my eyes!

There was Jack in the front row. "I know that guy!" I said. "That's Jack Berkowitz! I grew up with that guy! It's him, right?

Pappy's eyes clouded over. "You knew him?" He went on. "I hate to tell you this but Jack volunteered for a high altitude chamber test at Edwards in 1950. He suffered an aneurysm. They couldn't get him out in time. He was a really nice guy Pappy added. And smart too! Everyone sure liked him.

Mike Rizzi passed away from lung cancer, at 76, still smoking two packs a day. I had not seen him in 40 years.

Mule Ship

My cousin Bob went on to become one of the most successful ranchers in central Oregon but not without some unexpected events. Years after my summer in Fox valley I picked up a copy of Time magazine while working at the U.S. Army Yuma Test Station. The company I worked for, AeroJet General, had a contract to develop a surveillance drone and we were test flying early prototypes at the Test Range there. There was Bob's picture under the headline,

High Noon at Fox Valley.

I had heard nothing from my family but the article reported a gun duel between Bob and his brother-in-law, Linc. It seems that after Violet and her two brothers inherited the Fox Ranch it was divided, and the dispute arose when Linc tried to barricade the road across his acreage. There was no other way to get to Bob and Violet's section.

I remembered Linc, a very quiet fellow, had been drafted in 1940 only to be discharged a few weeks later. Of course at 14 I didn't ask any questions about this. We worked together that summer harvesting hay for the winter and slept in the same attic room without incident.

Over time Linc apparently became envious of Bob's success, and his own lack, and somehow decided he would take this action. The dispute went on for some time and Bob would simply tear down the barricade with Linc becoming ever more frustrated. He announced he would be there with a gun and stop any further access.

Figuring it was just a bluff Bob packed a rifle and as an afterthought a souvenir German Lugar and holster belt slung across his shoulder. Violet's older brother, George, was notified of this confrontation and arrived on the scene to mediate.

On that dirt road the three met with Linc finally agreeing to take the matter to court. As George and Bob turned to go back to their trucks Linc shot. The bullet grazed Bob's shirt just missing the Lugar hanging there. Bob thought he had been hit and whirled back grabbing the Lugar. The hair trigger on the automatic emptied the magazine. Three of the bullets found their mark in Linc's chest. He was dead.

Violet dutifully washed Bob's shirt.

A week in jail and then a trial. The decision was, self-defense------reasonable doubt prevailed.

Bob sold his collection of rifles and pistols.

Author's Note

Years later I figured it all out. How did the captain's boat get picked up in just four days? The emergency radio *was* working and they were able to have the SOS signal heard by a passing ship.

But why did the 2nd radio operator in our boat tell us otherwise? Not till 1995 and the Internet, was I able to find him and talk to him on the telephone. During that conversation he described how he was still the on boat deck when the ship broke in half. How was that so? Even in the darkness I was sure that the 2nd Mate followed me into boat #1 and the deck was clear. Our boat was at least ten yards off and moving away into the darkness when that happened. How could he have made it from the deck and to our boat? When I questioned him about this he could offer no explanation.

I could only conclude he was unreliable. But we made our decision based on his statement. Had we known, the following "Massive Search", as reported in the Western Australian newspaper on March 17th, 1945, would not have been required and maybe the death of seven navy airmen lost in a crashed search plane might have been avoided.

Dick Sproul

Search for Survivors of *SS Peter Silvester*, 10 February to 10 March, 1945—NARRATIVE:
(From U. S. Navy Archives)

1. On 10 February a signal was received from the *S.S. Cape Edmont* via Naval Board the she had rescued 15 survivors from the *S.S. Peter Silvester* which had been torpedoed in position 34 deg 19 min South 99 deg 37 min East at 1540Z on 6th February. The signal also stated that 3 boats and possibly 4 rafts were still afloat and that the aft part of the ship was still forming a menace to navigation.

2. C.S.W.P.S.F. promulgated a BAMS (British Allied Merchant Ships) message on 10 February that 3 boats and 4 rafts were adrift in the position indicated and that a portion of the ship presented a menace to navigation.

3. Shortly after receipt of *Cape Edmont* message H.M.A.S."*Dubbo* was recalled from the exercise area and she together with *USS Corpus Cristi* was prepared for a long search by topping up with fuel and fresh provisions to maximum capacity. *Corpus Cristi* proceeded out of the harbor at 0848Z /10th , followed by the *Dubbo* at 1135Z both with orders to proceed to the vicinity of the attack on *Peter Silvester* and endeavor to rescue survivors. Areas of search were suggested and a sketch of the suggested method of search was attached to the 'Sailing Orders.' Discretion was given regarding towing back or destroying the derelict if sighted, bearing in mind that survivors were the first importance. *Corpus Cristi* was to take charge of the operation. Arrangements had already been made with RAAF Headquarters for two Liberator Aircraft (stationed at CUNDERDIN) and an RAF Catalina to assist with the search from dawn SUNDAY 11th FEBRUARY. Further information received from *Cape Edmont* revealed that the survivors on board had been recovered in position 33 deg 34 min South 99 deg 08 min East. This information was passed to *Corpus Cristi* and *Dubbo* and authorities concerned, Throughout the operation ships searching, ships in the vicinity were kept informed of the daily situation.

Air searches:

(a) Two liberators East of line joining position 33 deg 47 min South 99 deg 05 min East and 32 deg 15 min South 99 deg 05 min East

(b) Catalina West of above line, Catalina was forced to return due to engine trouble.

Liberators searched for approximately two hours and sighted two rafts lashed together containing approximately 20men in pos 33 deg 05 min South 99 deg 10 min East. At 0005Z/ 11th. Supplies were dropped but it is doubtful the survivors could reach them as the parachute dragged the parcel a mile away. Weather at the time wind ENE 20 knots with high sea running. A signal was sent to *ASIS Darvel* informing her of the position of the rafts at 0005Z 11th and the estimated drift, This directed her to pass through the rescue position if she was not already ahead of it, keeping a good lookout for rafts and boats. C.S.W.P.S.F. and CinCE.I.S. were given this information and informed of the *Corpus Cristi* and *Dubbo* proceeding, the former probably arriving in the vicinity 1600Z 12th. It was suggested to CinC E.I. that a message be made on BAMS 7C to inform shipping. CinC EIS acting upon information contained in CSWPSF signal directed *HMS Slinger* and *Speaker* who were in passage from Colombo to Sydney to join in the search. *SS Cape Edmont* arrived Fremantle about midnight

11th. *Corpus Cristi* met *Cyrus T Brady* in position 32 deg 43 min South 110 deg 10 min East. This ship stated she had no survivors aboard.

12th FEBRUARY

Air Searches:

Two Liberators were briefed to search an area: 32 deg 50 min South 99 deg 10 min East, 33 deg 50 min South 99 deg 10 min East, 33 deg 50 min South 98 deg 10 min East and 32 deg 50 min South 98 deg 10 min East One Liberator was cancelled due to engine trouble the other proceeded. Results were negative apart from sighting of wreckage. *ASIS Darvel* was approaching the search position from the North and *Idomenus* from the South West. *Corpus Cristi* commenced searching at about 1200Z 12th. *Slinger* and *Speaker* were to the North West coming within search area early next morning. NOIC (F) told CinC EIS that he expected *Speaker* to shift to Baker Broadcast at 1200Z 13th although she would not at that time be within Baker area, in order to expedite passing information. Two Liberators searched slightly Northward of that on the previous day but sighted only wreckage. Information from survivors who were landed in FREMANTLE by *SS Cape Edmont* was to the effect that they reboarded the aft part of the ship after lying off for two days, all rafts 8 in number had then gone from the ship.

13 FEBRUARY

Air Searches:

(a) One Catalina was briefed to make a square search with center 33 deg 20 min S 98 deg 40 min E to endurance (about 7 hours in area)

(b) Two Liberators were briefed to search area: 33 deg 30 min S 98 deg 33 min E, 32 deg 40 min S 98 deg 33 min E, 32 deg 40 min S 97 deg 45 min E and 33 deg 20 min S 97 deg 45 min E. One Liberator became unserviceable.

Mule Ship

The second Liberator proceeded to search and sighted two rafts and one lifeboat and guided *Corpus Cristi* to them.

(c) *Slinger* and *Speaker* commenced to search area: 30 deg 31 min S 95 deg 35 min E, 29 deg 50 min S 97 deg 25 min E, 33 deg 00 min S 98 deg 45 min E and 33 deg 32 min S 97 deg 45 min E. *Corpus Cristi* picked up 62 survivors from four rafts lashed together in position 33 deg 14 min S 98 deg 30 min E at 0100ZZ 13th (Ed note: these were recovered before the Liberator sighting in time) In further signal he advised that he had on board 92 survivors including the Captain of the *Peter Silvester* recovered from 6 rafts and one lifeboat. *Darvel* carried out a short search in the area the proceeded to FREMANTLE. *Idomenus* steamed through the area and sighted abandoned boat which was original boat sighted by *Cape Edmont* from which 15 survivors were recovered.

HMS Slinger WIRE 21345 *Dubbo* entered the area PM having advised *Corpus Cristi* that her endurance for searching would be about one and a half to two days, gave her position course and speed and requested instructions.. CinC CEIS instructed carriers to read BAMS 5A and 7C while searching and *Slinger* reported her position as 30 deg 02 min S 96 deg 21 min E course 160 speed 16 knots at 0500Z 13th. NOICF congratulated the *Corpus Cristi* and asked for information on the two boats still missing. CTF71 assigned *Hutchinson* to NOICF who sailed this ship and *Warrnambool* to supplement search at 1224Z/13 and 1030Z/13 respectively. Both ships were given latest intelligence and search diagrams. *Corpus Cristi* reported the Master's estimated position of two boats unaccounted for if they were under sail was 28 deg 30 min S 103 deg 30 min E.

14 FEBRUARY

16. Air Searches

Dick Sproul

(a) two Liberators were briefed to search an area: 33 deg 00 min S 99 deg 05 min E, 33 deg 00 min S 98 deg 30 min E, 33 deg 40 min S 99 deg 20 min E and 33 deg 40 min S 99 deg 05 min E. One Liberator crashed on taking off resulting in five of the crew being killed. The second aircraft completed the search with negative results. Owing to the crash further participation by Liberators was cancelled.

(b) Carrier search 50 miles on each side of MLA 090 deg from position 33 deg 16 min S 96 deg 52 min E commencing at 2300Z 13th speed of advance 515 knots.

17. *Corpus Cristi* and *Dubbo* were still search the area. *Darvel* and *Idomenus* were proceeding to FREMANTLE and *Slinger* reported that sightings up to 0500Z/14th all within a 30 mile radius of position 33 deg 02min S 97 deg 54

min E. were as follows: *Corpus Cristi Dubbo* 1 empty life boat 6 empty rafts. Sundry wreckage and a number of horses (actually mules). *Slinger* advised proposed search on 15th. In view of this report it appeared the derelict after section had now sunk.

18. NOIC (F) asked CIC EI for the period carriers could remain and was told that they were to relinquish searching in time to reach SYDNEY at the end of February subject to CicC BPF concurring. BFP CinC later signaled concurrence amending arrival time to February 24th and 27th for *Speaker* and *Slinger* respectively. NOIC (F) then suggested the *Dubbo* de detached PM 15th. Returning to FREMANTLE with the survivors if *Corpus Cristi* concurred and later suggested of proposed searches for the 15th. And the area then being searched be considered clear and proposed that search should be made on 16th for two remaining boats commencing at position 31 deg 30 min S 103 deg 25 min E assuming the missing boats en route to AUSTRALIA.

19. *Warrnambool* advised her position at 2200Z/14 in view of altered scheme.

Mule Ship

15th FEBRUARY

20. Air Search

One Catalina was briefed to search area: (this search was later cancelled at 0400Z/15): 32 deg 40 min S 98 deg min E, 33 deg 20 min S 98 deg 33 min E, 33 deg 20 min S 97 deg 45 min E and 32 deg 40 min S 97 deg 45 min E.

(b) Carrier search 50 miles each side of line 090 deg MLA from position 32 deg 40 min S 96 deg 30 min E speed of advance 15 knots. Ships carried out surface sweep to the Eastward datum for next days search.

21. *Dubbo* and *Corpus Cristi* had by then found the carriers and *Dubbo* refueled from *Speaker* AM 15th thus to cancelled proposed return to FREMANTLE. *Dubbo* proceeded to carry out search of the area outlined for Catalina search and *Corpus Cristi* remained as screen for carriers.

22. NOIC (F) asked for carriers intentions and told *Slinger* to plan further searches bearing in mind the time left. CinC BPF was asked for a firm date for carriers to arrive in SYDNEY.

23. *Corpus Cristi* and *Hutchinson* and *Warrnambool* to proceed to position 31 deg 30 min S 103 deg 25 min E and search line of 050 from that position.

NOIC (F) cancelled *Warrnambool*'s participation in the search (advising *Corpus Cristi* Accordingly) and directed him to search area of projected Catalina search.

24. CinC BPF agreed to carriers search continuing subject to their conforming with arrival dates as previously mentioned in CinC EI concurred in the search projected for the 16th.

25. *Slinger* detached *Corpus Cristi* at 1100Z/15 with instructions to pass through the area outlined and then proceed to FREMANTLE. NOIC (F) approved this.

26. NOIC (F) told DUBBO to search area: 29 deg 52 min S 104 deg 06 min E, 30 deg 50 min S 102 deg 47 min E,

Dick Sproul

30 deg 04 min S 102 deg 06 min E and 28 deg 11 min S 103 deg 13 min E and *Warrnambool'* to search area 065 deg from line joining position 28 deg 39 min S 106 deg 06 min E and 27 deg 15 min S 105 deg 30 min E to endurance. All ships were advised that the Catalina search would be carried out on the 16th.

27 *Slinger* advised the he proposed searching in company with *Speaker* on 16th, detaching *Speaker* for SYDNEY on conclusion of days operation and continuing alone on 17th, and 18th and asked for more shore based aircraft search Eastward of his area.

28. Air Search

(a) One Catalina was briefed to carry out the search proposed for the 15th. Shore based aircraft to seaward of in this ea ceased after this operation.

(b) Carrier search 50 miles each side of line 050 deg MLA from position 31 deg 30 min D 103 deg 25 min E This was later terminated at position 29 deg 40 min S 105 deg 50 min E and a further area added as follows: (c) 29 deg 05 min S 105 deg 50 min E by 28 deg 20 min S 107 deg 35 min E by (d) 29 deg 05 min S 108 deg 00 min E by 30 deg 05 min S 106 deg 20 min E.

29. CinC BPF amended *Slinger* due date at SYDNEY to 25th and NOIMC (f) asked *Slinger* for his intentions, telling Hutchinson to remain with *Slinger* as consort on 17th. *Slinger* gave her estimated position at 2300Z/16 (26 deg 40

min 1o7 deg 15 min E course 107 speed 15 knots) to *Hutchinson* and told her

to join him, then cancelled projected search for 17th and 18th substituting a further area for 17th.

30. In view of this NOIC(F) ordered *Hutchinson* to search area below on completion of operation of 17th. 30 deg 05 min S 106 deg 48 min E by 28 deg 50 min S 105 deg 30 min E by 27 deg 42 min S by 107 deg 05 \min E by 28 deg 55 min S 108 deg 28 min E.

31. *Dubbo* was by this time in her search area, the Catalina had completed with negative results, *Warrnambool* was in her area and *Hutchinson* was in the Western area covered by carriers on 16th. *Corpus Cristi* was through the search area and headed for FREMANTLE.

32. Actually *Hutchinson* was unable to make the rendezvous as signaled by *Slinger* so steered to intercept on the run south. *Slinger* advised that she could not contact *Hutchinson* and NOIC(F) broadcast the purport of *Slinger* messages. The actual position of the *Hutchinson* was not known until some time later. The days operation was negative.

17 FEBRUARY

33. Air Search: Carriers 50 miles either side of line 135 degrees MLA from position 26 deg 0 min S min E for 150 miles. *Warrnambool* gave her position at 0100z/17TH AS 26 DEG 40 MINS 108 DEG 44 MIN E course 010 deg speed 9 knots until 0500Z/17 thence a course 135 deg to daylight 18th.

34. *Slinger* advised the air search has been abandoned after 30 miles due to unfavorable conditions and that she was continuing Surface search along MLA during daylight thence proceeding to SYDNEY via point A on her original route.

35, NOIC(F) directed *Castlemaine* due FREMANTLE on 23 from DARWIN to pass through 27 deg 56 min S 111 deg 16 min E and 31 deg52 min S 114 deg 22 min E warning her to keep a lookout for the missing boats and Coastal Authorities as far north ad DERBY were warned to keep a lookout for missing boats.

36, *Hutchinson* asked for *Slinger's* position and NOIC(F) told her to report her whereabouts and told *Warrnambool* to search as previously ordered. *Slinger* gave her midnight position as 29 deg 42 min S 110 deg 10 min E and advised she had not contacted *Hutchinson*. *Hutchinson* reported her position at 1200Z/17th as 27 deg 32 min 106 deg 49 min E course 180 deg speed 15 knots.

18 FEBRUARY

37. Air Search nil.

38. NOIC(F) told *Hutchinson* to search area 27 deg 33 min S 106 deg 57 min E .

39. *Warrnambool* reported weather unsuitable for northerly run and was told to proceed at discretion but a search South of 245 degs from GERALDTON was not considered useful.

40. *Hutchinson* proceeded to new area having carried out a short search of the area assigned to *Warrnambool*. *Dubbo* continued searching her area.

19 FEBRUARY

41. AIR SEARCH: Two Beauforts were briefed to search the coast from GERALDTON to PORT REDLAND carrying out a box search to a depth of 100 miles off North West Cape returning the next day. Air search was negative.

42. *Dubbo* reported her position as 29 deg 52 min S 104 deg 06 min E at 0100Z/19th, and she could stay in the area until 1000Z on 20th and was told by NOIC(F) to return to FREMANTLE keeping North of 30 deg S until 110 deg E using wide zigzag until then.

43. *Hutchinson* continued searching her area and *Warrnambool* was about 120 miles South West of GERALDTON working to the southward.

20 FEBRUARY

44. AIR SEARCH :Two Beauforts returned from REDLAND TO GERALDTON doing a box search to a depth of 100 miles of North West Cape. Result was negative.

45. NOIUC thanked the carriers and advised them that some of the survivors had seen their aircraft and were greatly impressed with their search. NOIC(F) then

abandoned the search but arranged for a repetition of the Beaufort search of 19 and 20th on 25th and 26th.

23 FEBRUARY

48. *Castlemaine* reported nil sightings. 25th and 26th
49. and 50. Air search by Beauforts negative.

28 FEBRUARY

51. *HMS Activity* reported picking up 20 survivors of *Peter Silvester* from 1 lifeboat bound for AUSTRALIA in position 26 deg 48 min S 101 deg 58 min E at 0440Z on 28th and CinC EI ordered *Formidable* and *Uganda* to pass through this area and carry out a search in passing.

2 MARCH

52. *HMS Activity* landed survivors in FREMANTLE who stated remaining boat also headed for AUSTRALIA.

3 MARCH

53. *Formidable* arrived FREMANTLE and reported Search negative.

4 MARCH

54. *Uganda* arrived FREMANTLE and reported search negative.

10 MARCH

55. On the morning *USS ROCK* picked up the remaining boat from the *Peter Silvester* with 15 survivors 20 miles West of VLAMING HD Light NORTH WEST CAPE. Survivors were in fair condition with the exception of one man who needed hospital treatment. (Charles Kemmer)

Dick Sproul

Thanks to David Stevens, who wrote the U-Boat Far from Home published by Allen and Unwin in 1997. Stevens writes much from the view of the German Crew using the personal log of the first officer as a guide.

In June of 1944 the U-Boat left Bergen, Norway and headed North along the coast but tied up in Trondhiem to fix an oil leak. The boat then left a second time north to skirt the Arctic ice pack and sortie through the Denmark straits. She gradually made her way down the center of the Atlantic under orders to avoid contact. Captain Timm took the boat South past the equator, and found its first victim Robin Goodfellow. By August U-862 was in the Mozambique Channel between Madagascar and African mainland where four more merchant ships were sent to the bottom. Thence the U-862 after an encounter with a Catalina aircraft, Captain Timm decided to head directly to the base at Penang in Malaya.

The *U862* next patrol was to take it down past Western Australia and thence through the Bight and to the Sydney area where it sank the Liberty ship *Robert Weaver*. Timm next headed around New Zealand and then retracing its outward path back to Penang. Unfortunately it encountered one more ship the Liberty ship *Peter Silvester* (Peter Silvester was a New York Congressman from 1847-1851).

To the liberty ship *Peter Silvester* fell the dubious privilege of being the last allied ship sunk by enemy action in the Indian Ocean. The night of the attack was dark. The ship's crew of 42, 26 USN Armed Guard, and 106 servicemen as passengers had no warning. About 2140 the first salvo of two torpedoes struck starboard in Number 3 hold putting out all lights and communication out of order. The second attack was a half an hour after the first when two more torpedoes struck. The ship was ordered abandoned, but while this activity was starting a final fifth torpedo hit the

Mule Ship

bow, breaking the ship in two, with the bow sinking immediately.

(Author's note: This account differs from what I witnessed. The ship breaking up may have sounded like torpedo hits to survivors further away. Also I saw only one flash and explosion while on the boat deck just before lowering the boats. After that no further torpedoes struck) In all 32 men were lost in the sinking and from wounds.

The first officer's journal final entry "Secure in Shonan. End of war cruise in East Asia. We Live." "We live" might well be the motto for all that survived

Dick Sproul

The 'E' Ticket

When Disneyland first opened, about 1954 I think it was, the admission price included a book of tickets good for the rides available at the new park. There were six or eight "A" tickets, good for the little kiddie rides and some of the carnival type rides. The B, C, and D tickets were for rides or attractions of ascending value but descending quantity, and with longer lines. But the four "E" tickets in the back of the book, they were for the very best, most thrilling, scary, exciting rides; the Matterhorn Mountain, The Jungle Safari, It's a Small World and others. Ah, the "E" tickets, they were for the rides everyone wanted!

"Hurry! Before the line gets any longer!"--- "Keep your hands and elbows inside the car."

But now at 84 years I have to say my life has been an "E" ticket! My grandfather warned me, and he was right of course, that "life is full of hard knocks." But even so what a grand ride it's been!

Sure enough, there were often times in life when B and C type events come up (along with the boring equivalent of standing in long lines (or the disappointment of having the "ride" close up just as you were ready to get on.) And sure, even quite a few "A" ticket events. But like I said, oh!

Those E ticket rides!

I just wish I could do it all over again. Well, not all of it.

I'll leave it to you to decide which rides I would like to do again.

Dick Sproul

Mule Ship

Joan

I first saw her at IngleAirs. A young peoples club sponsored by the city of Inglewood, California.--- Like it was yesterday. She came off the dance floor and the fellow she was with said a few words and then walked away leaving her standing there alone in the doorway, thick dark curls tumbling to her shoulders, She looked a little lost. I thought what a fool that fellow was. I would never walk away from a girl like that!

She wasn't just pretty; she was different, interesting. And a well filled out sweater and skirt and the smallest waist.

Standing at the drink bar I turned to Pat, a friend "Who is that?" I asked her.

"That's Joan Regan, she's from Boston. Would you like to meet her?"

Oh Yes - I - would. -------

There were beach parties, ski trips and a big Luau that we all worked so hard to put on.

A year and a half later we were married in Sun Valley Idaho, while on an IngleAirs ski trip.

And then a whole year in the San Francisco Bay area. We spent every weekend exploring. The bridges, the ferryboats, and in Oakland the First and Last Chance Saloon. It had been Jack London's hangout. Lombard street. The India House, a restaurant so exotic. And Bibo's 365 club. There seemed to be a real live nude girl in a small fish tank rotating on a pedestal, Finochios, where beautifully dressed women entertained---- but were actually men.

Dick Sproul

Joan could not believe it! Nothing like that in Boston! There were trips to Yosemite and Monterey. A yearlong adventure.

I said she was different, I was to find out how different!

Her modesty was not false. Her honesty and openness was refreshing and always kept things interesting.

We teased her about her Boston accent.

She learned to dance with me and ski with me. She worked so hard to make things good. Her first Thanksgiving turkey really wasn't bad.

We had two beautiful baby girls that we played with and loved and who loved us back.

And then three years in Yuma, Arizona, when the kids were small. What a change! 115 degrees! In the shade! But I remember the fun we had helping stage a little theater production, "Three men on a horse" an old Broadway play.

Then back to California, Garden Grove and then Mission Viejo. Our girls went to the San Juan Capistrano Mission School, played softball, competed on the swim team.

And when our two wonderful daughters were grown Joan often traveled with me on my business trips. I landed a job in Germany where I had to visit different Army posts. We always remembered the night we spent in an attic room in Mienz, Germany. There was a trade show and it was the only room we could find. No heat and two tiny beds on the coldest night. We finally snuggled in one bed with all the blankets and managed to not fall on the floor.

Then Cliff and Mary Boehmer, our neighbors who came over from Mision Viejo, spent a month with us. On long weekends the four of us saw Salzburg, Rome and Florence and the Octoberfest in Munich. We visited the Austrian and German Alps.

Mule Ship

Then on my second trip to Germany a year and a half later, we visited Cliff and Mary's son Rick and his wife Diana in Paris. Rick's law firm had opened an office there. Diana, who had learned to speak French, took us on a two day tour like no other.

We skied the Alps. Kaprun in Austria and Jungfrau in the German Alps. Castles and Weinstubes and the torch lit castle in Heidelberg. We lived for seven months in Ochsenfurt a small medieval village on the Main river. It had stone walls and even a mote. And the Rathouse, (that's the city hall) the Metzgeri, (the butcher shop) the bakeri, (bakery). Our landlords, Heidi and Wolfgang, dear people who took us on a volksmarch and to dinner at a working German farm where I practiced my German. Schnapps and snitzel, wiesswurst and wiesswien and those delicious freshly baked rolls that we took home for breakfast.

We spent five months in Hawaii, where I worked at Schofield Barracks. We went exploring or scuba diving on weekends. Of course I should also mention the few weeks in Killeen, Texas, at Ft. Hood and yes, even in Tacoma at Ft. Lewis.

And then Yakima. So many wonderful people. What a nice place to be. Wherever we went Joan was the magnet that drew our friends. So loyal, so fierce in defense of our children, and yes, our grand children.

Too trusting at times, but quick to spot a phony

Accurate with her insight, yet at times quaintly, a little naive and so even more endearing. She really was the wind beneath my wings. And my compass too, always keeping me pointed in the right direction. I would surely have crashed to earth without her. Through good times and bad, she was always there for me.

Dick Sproul

I remember a Gypsy fortuneteller we visited in San Francisco. The Gypsy told Joan that we would have a home and have children. And then she told her that we would never be rich. We would never be poor but we would never be rich.

That Gypsy was so wrong-- Joan made me--- the richest man on earth.

Mule Ship

Dick Sproul

Acknowledgements

As a world-class procrastinator it took the gentle nudging of publisher, author and friend, Al Allaway to finally get this completed. Without his help this book might never have gone to print. I am also grateful to all the members of the YakWriters Club here in Yakima, Washington. They provided that rare quality, unbiased critique and expert knowledge so valuable. I wish I had the space to name them all.

And thanks to Susan Caruso for her valuable editing and advice, and for tracking down all those many small errors.

I also want to thank Charis Dawson for her loving support as well as a comfortable place to live and work. I will ever be grateful for the lucky day we met.

Dick Sproul